Standards
and
Mastery Learning

**CORWIN
PRESS**

The Corwin Press logo—a raven striding across an open book—represents the happy union of courage and learning. We are a professional-level publisher of books and journals for K-12 educators, and we are committed to creating and providing resources that embody these qualities. Corwin's motto is "Success for All Learners."

Standards *and* Mastery Learning

Aligning Teaching and Assessment
So All Children Can Learn

J. Ronald Gentile
James P. Lalley

CORWIN PRESS, INC.
A Sage Publications Company
Thousand Oaks, California

For information:

Corwin Press, Inc.
A Sage Publications Company
2455 Teller Road
Thousand Oaks, California 91320
www.corwinpress.com

Sage Publications Ltd.
6 Bonhill Street
London EC2A 4PU
United Kingdom

Sage Publications India Pvt. Ltd.
B-42, Panchsheel Enclave
Post Box 4109
New Delhi 110 017 India

Printed in the United States of America

Library of Congress Cataloging-in-Publication Data

Library of Congress Cataloging-in-Publication Data
Gentile, J. Ronald (James Ronald), 1941-
Standards and mastery learning: Aligning teaching and assessment so all children can learn / J. Ronald Gentile, James P. Lalley.
        p. cm.
Includes bibliographical references and index.
ISBN 0-7619-4614-4 (C) -- ISBN 0-7619-4615-2 (P) 1.   Mastery learning-United States. 2.   Education-Standards-United States. I. Lalley, James P. II. Title.
LB1031.4 .G46 2003
371.39—dc21   2002151362

This book is printed on acid-free paper.

03   04   05   06   07   7   6   5   4   3   2   1

Acquisitions Editor:	Rachel Livsey
Editorial Assistant:	Phyllis Cappello
Production Editor:	Melanie Birdsall
Typesetter:	C&M Digitals (P) Ltd.
Copy Editor:	Carla Freeman
Indexer:	Sheila Bodell
Cover Designer:	Michael Dubowe
Production Artist:	Janet Foulger

Contents

Preface   vii
About the Authors   xiii

1. Understanding Mastery Learning   1
   The Learning/Memory Base   2
   The Measurement Base   5
   Theoretical Bases   9
   The Brain Base   12
   The Empirical Base   15
   Discussion and Conclusions   18
   Summary   20

2. Examining the Standards: Math,
   Science, Social Studies, and English Language Arts   23
   Mastery as a Beginning   24
   Beyond Mastery   25
   Mathematics Standards   34
   Science Standards   44
   Social Studies Standards   54
   English Language Arts Standards   66
   Summary   80

3. Planning Standards-Based
   Lessons Using Mastery Learning   83
   Overlap Among State and National Standards   83
   Enrichment and Remediation   92
   Planning Lessons Using
      Six Elements of Mastery Learning   95
   Summary   118

4. Implementing Standards and
   Mastery Learning in the Classroom   121
   Implementing Mastery Learning: 13 Steps   121
   Summary   129

5. Professional Development and Mastery Learning   131

    The Misadventures of Mastery Learning   131

    Professional Development of Teachers   135

    Mastery Learning: A Plan for Action and a
       Professional Development Agenda   146

    Teaching for Mastery: All Children Can Learn   151

    Summary   152

Appendix: What Does the Literature Tell Us?   155

    Two Approaches to Mastery Learning   155

    Defining Features of Mastery Learning   156

    Empirical Evidence: Overview and Executive Summary   157

    Research Examples   160

    Memory by Fast and Slow Learners   162

    What Are the Effects of Mastery on Teachers?   165

Glossary   169

References   177

Author Index   185

Subject Index   187

Preface

"Education isn't what it used to be, but then it never was," Mark Twain was reported to have joked. He might have said the same thing about "standards." Like education in general, standards either supply the promise of a better future or are the root of our problems, depending on the side of the political landscape on which you stand. Perhaps Benjamin Barber (1992) asked the hardest question: "What are we to make of a society that deploys rigorous standards of culture and learning in its schools which are nowhere to be found in the practices and behavior of the society itself?" (pp. 215-216).

And yet, when work is shoddy, food is contaminated, or air travel is unsafe, the public clamors for higher standards. It is the American way of complaining, yes, but it is also the American way of pulling ourselves up by our bootstraps. So it seems natural when education is perceived as ailing or failing that we turn to standards as our solution.

The history of standards in America is long and tortuous (for a good, brief history see Marzano & Kendall, 1996). It includes at least one notable success, defined as widespread adoption, in the invention of "the Carnegie unit" in the early 20th century, which standardized the meaning of course credit in terms of class time. The history also includes such notable failures as "the new math," which rewrote mathematics curricula in response to the Soviet Union's launching of Sputnik in midcentury. It failed and was eventually replaced with a back-to-basics movement. As Linus (in the "Peanuts" comic strip) quipped, "How can you do new math with an old math mind?"

The history of standards also reflects federal government versus states' rights skirmishes, competition among professional organizations (for what will be required and what will be optional for graduation), religious versus secular issues, as well as numerous other political issues beyond the scope of this book.

What does seem relevant, however, is an apparent shift in the goals of standards from inputs to outputs, in Marzano and Kendall's (1996) shorthand. Whereas previous standards emphasized what had to go into a course (specifics of the curriculum, how material was to be taught, how many credits or Carnegie units it was worth), current standards emphasize what comes out (what students know or can do and how to assure accountability). As Marzano and Kendall (1996) summarized, "The new, more efficient and accountable view of education is output-based; success is defined in terms of students learning specific standards" (p. 17).

Whether the "outputs" view is better or worse, we cannot be sure, though it certainly created a firestorm of rhetoric over the high-stakes testing, perhaps a too-narrow view of accountability that has become linked to the standards movement beginning in the 1980s. Interestingly, the input/output categories have rough parallels with fundamental variables in John Carroll's (1963) model of school learning, which provides some of the theoretical underpinnings of mastery learning. Those variables are opportunity and perseverance. *Opportunity*, in rough parallel to input, is the time allowed or scheduled by the teacher to cover the material and induce students to learn. *Perseverance*, in rough analogy to output, is the time the students spend or are willing to spend to learn. Although both of these are important to and predictive of achievement, perseverance becomes the bottom line: Teachers have been successful to the extent that they induce students to do what they need to do to learn.

We bring this up here to point out that the mastery philosophy on which this book is based is potentially compatible with current views of standards, but it has developed methods for measuring and motivating students to persevere until they achieve those standards. Sadly, many advocates of standards, not to mention those who are charged with implementing them, know little or nothing about implementing mastery learning: its philosophy, its evolution, what makes it work or undermines it, its varieties. Thus, although the movement toward higher academic standards carries with it assumptions about learning, development, and measurement that have traditionally been central to the theory and philosophy of mastery learning, the standards movement has neither embraced mastery learning nor shown evidence of having learned from its successful or unsuccessful practices.

In this text, we describe the various foundations on which mastery learning is built—the learning/memory base, the measurement base, the empirical base, and various theoretical bases—and argue that if the standards movement does not build on these foundations, we may be witnessing history repeating itself as "déjà vu all over again."

After establishing that the "new standards" are fundamentally based on the principles of mastery learning, we will examine national and state standards and relate them specifically to mastery. The remainder of the text is dedicated to providing ways for educators to assist students in meeting the standards.

Intended Audience

This book is intended for prospective and current teachers, principals and staff developers, and teacher educators. We understand that each of these classes of professionals looks at an educational idea from a somewhat different perspective: teachers, from the point of view of the idea's practicality and usefulness in the context of all they are required to do already; administrators and staff developers, in terms of resources and accountability; and teacher educators/professors of education, from the vantage point of its theoretical viability and empirical support. And yet all would agree that they have no time to waste on ideas that do not help students learn.

As teacher educators ourselves, we wish to reach each of these audiences. Thus in this book, we have done our best to (a) provide practical and usable ideas about mastery learning and (b) explain how to implement it in the context of a theoretical perspective, including assessing its effectiveness in achieving the standards that we as a society have set for ourselves. Finally, we have presented the evidence in a general way in the text, while providing more details (for those who wish to pursue both evidence and the methodological issues that accompany such evidence) in the Appendix.

Acknowledgments

Appreciation is expressed to Dr. Kay Johnson-Gentile for her suggestions and reflections throughout the preparation of this manuscript, as well as for permission to reprint portions of her course syllabus.

Special thanks are due to Namisi Chilungu, Nicole Robinson, and Brenna Towle for permission to use excerpts of their lessons and personal experiences, and to Dr. Marianne Baker for the data on which Table 1.2 is based.

Many thanks also to Gina Pannozzo and Kathleen Lesniak for their comments on portions of this book, and to Peggy Lyons and Shelly Cohen for their word processing assistance in initial stages of the writing.

The contributions of the following reviewers are also gratefully acknowledged:

Pauline Schara
Principal
Linda Vista Elementary
Yorba Linda, CA

RoseAnne O'Brien Vojtek
Principal
Ivy Drive Elementary School
Bristol, CT

Joseph Peake
Executive Director
Central Coast California School Leadership Center
Santa Barbara, CA

Charlie F. Adamchik Jr.
Teacher/Educational Consultant
Blairsville-Saltsburg School District
Blairsville, PA

Lorin W. Anderson
Carolina Distinguished Professor of Education
University of South Carolina
Columbia, SC

Allan A. Glatthorn
Professor Emeritus
School of Education
East Carolina University
Greenville, NC

Bob Marzano
Adjunct Professor, Cardinal Stritch University
Milwaukee, WI
Senior Scholar
McREL (Mid-Continent Research for Education and Learning)
Aurora, CO

Dr. Pearl Solomon
Professor Emeritus
St. Thomas Aquinas College
Sparkill, NY

David Scheidecker
Academic Facilitator
Neuqua Valley High School
Naperville, IL

The following national organizations are also acknowledged for permission to quote from their standards (particularly in Chapter 2):

Reprinted with permission from the Principles and Standards for School Mathematics (2000) by the National Council of Teachers of Mathematics. All rights reserved.

Reprinted with permission from the National Science Education Standards (1996) by the National Academy Press.

Reprinted with permission from Expectations of Excellence: Curriculum Standards for Social Studies (1994) by the National Council for the Social Studies.

Standards for the English Language Arts, by the International Reading Association and the National Council of Teachers of English, Copyright 1996 by the International Reading Association and the National Council of Teachers of English. Reprinted with permission.

About the Authors

 **J. Ronald Gentile** is a graduate of Penn State University (B.S., 1963, and M.S., 1964, in Psychology; and Ph.D., in 1967, in Educational Psychology) and has been teaching educational psychology at the University at Buffalo, State University of New York, since 1969. Among his more than threescore publications are the following continuing research interests: memory by fast versus slow learners; mastery learning, standards, and grading policies; and expanding the instructional repertoire. For Dr. Gentile and his wife, Dr. Kay Johnson-Gentile ("The Genteels"), expanding the instructional repertoire has included teaching teachers how to integrate music into the elementary school curriculum. In 1998, Dr. Gentile was promoted to the rank of SUNY Distinguished Teaching Professor.

 **James P. Lalley** is an Assistant Professor of Education at D'Youville College in Buffalo, New York. He is a graduate of the State University of New York at Buffalo (B.A., 1984, in History; and M.A., 1995, and Ph.D., 1997, in Educational Psychology). He has taught at the State University of New York, College at Buffalo and Canisius College. His previous publications have been in the areas of educational technology and child development. In addition to mastery learning, his professional interests include how affective factors influence motivation and learning, methods of teaching, and children at risk.

1

Understanding Mastery Learning

The movement toward higher academic standards for our children carries with it a number of implications, some explicit, some implied:

- That there is some consensus on our academic goals and priorities

- That those goals are both explicable and measurable

- That we can validly differentiate between truly competent, incompetent, or incomplete achievement in those academic domains

- That we have the resources and the will to remediate and motivate those who are initially unprepared for, or slow to grasp, one or more of those academic goals

- That in attaining those new higher standards, we model fair and equitable procedures

It is our thesis that all the above points are intimately connected to mastery learning (and criterion-referenced assessment). Indeed, the standards for each of the professional disciplines are amply stocked with phrases such as "All children can learn," "Aim for mastery," and "Students should be able to demonstrate competent levels of achievement."

The problem is that although the connection between teaching to standards and mastery learning is logical and natural, only a small proportion of teachers and schools have adopted mastery learning. Moreover, many of those who claim to be using mastery learning make one or more of the following common, often fatal, mistakes: (a) Passing a mastery test is conceptualized as the endpoint instead of the initial stage of the learning/memory process; (b) there is no requirement and concomitant grading incentive to go beyond initial mastery; (c) mastery testing is embedded in an overall grading scheme (often a leftover norm-referenced and competitive scheme) that contradicts the goal of achieving mastery by all (a criterion-referenced purpose); (d) demonstrations of mastery are limited to objective tests at the knowledge/recall end of the thinking continuum (e.g., Bloom's 1956 taxonomy); and therefore (e) students are overtested and underchallenged.

The above errors are common, we believe, because educators tend to think of mastery learning as a teaching technique or a testing procedure, instead of a philosophy or theory that provides the basis for decisions about techniques or assessments. Furthermore, they do not understand the theoretical and empirical bases on which mastery learning is founded.

It is our purpose in this introductory chapter to briefly describe each of the following foundations for mastery learning: the learning/memory base, the measurement base, the theoretical bases (including competency vs. helplessness, Erikson's social development theory, and Carroll's model), the brain base, and the empirical base. The accumulated weight of these positions will lead us to some conclusions about teaching, assessment, and grading. These, in turn, will be directly relevant to the standards movement of our time and why these new standards will fail if we do not take heed of the lessons from mastery learning.

The Learning/Memory Base

Consider a learning task: memorizing multiplication facts or vocabulary; acquiring a skill, such as playing a piece on the piano or hitting a tennis ball with topspin; comprehending a paragraph or theory; or learning a new teaching technique or thinking strategy. Each of these, from the simplest to the most complex, has a number of essential prerequisites—that is, some prior knowledge that if previously acquired and currently activated can facilitate achievement of

Figure 1.1   The S-Shaped Learning Curve

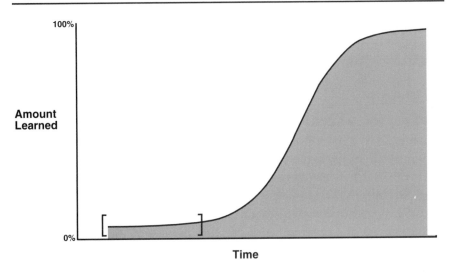

the task at hand. For multiplication facts, two likely essentials are one-to-one correspondence for rational counting, and skill with addition. For thinking strategies, metacognitive skills (such as the ability to actively monitor what you comprehend and what you don't) and the ability to organize and categorize are likely prerequisites. If such prior knowledge or skill is absent, then the learning task is more difficult. And to complete the scenario, if the prerequisite knowledge has been mislearned or is otherwise inaccurate, acquisition of the new task is further confounded with the need to unlearn prior misconceptions.

Teachers acknowledge the differences in prior learning among their charges in regard to their *readiness*. We speak of Mary, who has great facility for foreign languages, or Bill, who is not yet ready to read. In the terminology of the famous *S*-shaped learning curve (see Figure 1.1), readiness is manifested in how long the line is before any progress or acceleration can be observed. Students like Mary, who have mastered prerequisites, may show immediate progress, whereas students like Bill may need hours or days trying to figure out what the task is or to acquire the prerequisites, and thus remain in the bracketed part of the curve for an extended period.

Learning, in other words, occurs in phases or episodes, and this *original learning phase* includes (a) the readiness component (described above), (b) learning to initial mastery, and (c) forgetting. Although forgetting has not been mentioned up to now, it is clear that forgetting is the inevitable result of initial learning, even when a high mastery standard of, say, 80% to 100% correct is required. When the degree of original learning is less than mastery, say, 60% to 80%, then forgetting is likely to occur more rapidly or be more complete. If it is less than 60%, it is questionable to speak of forgetting at all, because learning was inadequate in the first place.[1]

Students show that they understand this principle implicitly when they ask, "Why do we have to learn this stuff anyway? We'll only forget it." Our typical answers, "Because it will be on the test" or "Because I said so," are not satisfactory. In fact, we have been able to find only one satisfactory answer to the question, and it was supplied in one of the first empirical studies of learning/forgetting (Ebbinghaus, 1885/1964). The answer is that relearning is faster—that is, there is a considerable *savings* of time in relearning compared with original learning. Furthermore, there is a positive relationship between amount of time saved in relearning and the degree of original learning, with essentially no savings when original learning is below some acceptable threshold (which we earlier argued was 60% or less).

If original acquisition and forgetting constitute Phase 1 of learning, then each new relearning and forgetting episode constitutes an additional phase. In addition, for material or skills that were mastered in Phase 1, each new relearning episode constitutes additional amounts of *overlearning*, defined as practice beyond initial learning, which is inversely related to forgetting.

Each new relearning-forgetting phase also provides the opportunity for *distributed practice*—that is, rehearsal of the material over hours, days, and weeks. When compared with *massed practice* (i.e., cramming, or including the same number of learning episodes into one session), the positive effects of distributed practice on memory are widely known, as advertised by teachers and coaches when they say, "Practice a little each day." From a cognitive constructivist point of view, distributed practice also provides experience retrieving previously stored material, comparing new examples with those stored, reorganizing what is known, and recoding it for memory storage and subsequent accessibility.

Although the above material has been widely known for decades and documented in many basic learning as well as educational psychology texts,[2] it is not usually considered in the context of mastery learning. And yet the implications are straightforward and powerful, as both a positive and a negative example will portray.

For the positive example, consider the experience we teachers have. The first year of teaching a unit, we have a lot to learn (even though many prerequisites have already been mastered in college and student teaching). The next year, when we reach that unit again, we find we've forgotten quite a bit. Fortunately, relearning is faster, and we find ourselves reorganizing the material, coming up with new examples, and so forth. The next year, forgetting has been less yet, and thus there is greater savings in relearning. By the 10th year, the material is almost totally recalled, with examples virtually falling off the tongue. The material seems so easy by this time that many teachers can now be heard complaining, "The students are getting dumber and dumber every year." Sadly, this is one of the negative effects of becoming expert in something: We lose empathy for the novice. (Note the parallel to what happens once a nonconserver on Piaget's tasks becomes a conserver: e.g., the 8-year-old who understands that the amount of water does not change when poured into a taller, thinner glass cannot recall that she expected more in the taller, thinner glass when she was 5). This is also what distinguishes a mere expert from a teacher: An expert can do it; a teacher can do it but also remembers what it takes to progress from novice to expert.

For the negative example of how these learning/memory concepts form the basis for mastery learning, consider some students whose original learning is 50% or less. Their forgetting in Phase 1 will be at least as rapid as it will for those who mastered the material and, because they learned so little, more complete. Furthermore, there will be little or no savings in relearning during Phase 2. Then, if this material is treated as a review ("This was covered last year"), less time will be spent on relearning (and after all, students who mastered originally will need less time). Thus the relearning episode for those who need it most will also be substandard, leading to relatively little residue in memory and therefore little or no savings for Phase 3 relearning. By Phase 3, the motivation to learn this material will also be eroding ("I was never very good at this"), an issue we shall explore in more detail in "Learned Helplessness."

A summary of the long-term effects of the difference between mastery and nonmastery at original learning is provided in Figure 1.2. After four or five episodes, when learners in Part A say to those in Part B, "I forgot more than you ever learned," the sad fact will be that they are telling the truth. A close look at the curve in Part B shows that after four or five episodes, those persons—they can hardly be called learners—have learning/forgetting curves that resemble the brain waves of comatose patients.

The Measurement Base

Since at least Glaser's (1963; Glaser & Nitko, 1971) publications, the field of educational measurement has acknowledged the importance

Figure 1.2   Hypothetical Learning/Forgetting Curves for Mastery Versus Nonmastery

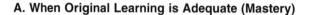

A. When Original Learning is Adequate (Mastery)

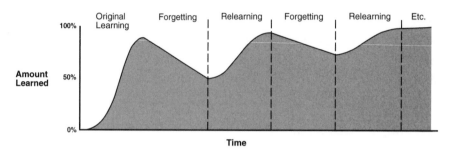

B. When Original Learning is Inadequate (Nonmastery)

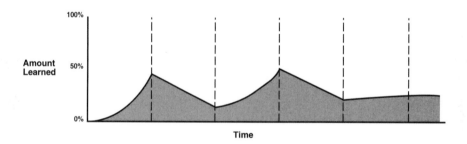

of the distinction between *norm-referenced* (NR) and *criterion-referenced* (CR) assessment. Whereas NR assessment is used to refer to the traditional psychometric approach of measuring and comparing individual differences in relation to norms provided by others, CR assessment interprets a student's score in relation to the goals and criteria of instruction without regard to other students' scores.

NR assessment, therefore, is useful for obtaining rank in class, for estimating a person's status in relation to some normative group, and for selecting the most qualified people from a long list of hopefuls (for awards, for graduate school, etc.). CR assessment, in contrast, is useful for measuring how skillful a person is in relation to a particular instructional domain, what growth a person has demonstrated over time, and what else the person needs to attain specified instructional goals. In Bloom's (1976) succinct contrast, it is a difference between selecting talent and developing talent.

For NR purposes, students take a test or perform a skill and are scored relative to one another or to appropriate norms. The absolute score is not important and is usually not even meaningful, for at least the following reasons. First, the domain being tested is not usually clearly specified and does not have to be. To rank people on IQ or math aptitude, for example, it is best to write items that sample from many areas, not just vocabulary or exponents. Second, to maximize reliability of measurement, each item selected for the test should be missed by about 50% of the examinees; this maximizes the range of the test scores and creates a normal curve. Scores on the test, therefore, are not interpretable, except in relation to the norms; for example, hearing that your child scored 430 on the SAT verbal test tells you nothing about what questions he or she could answer, and indeed, this information needs to be accompanied by statistics such as percentile rank (e.g., 38th percentile) to have any meaning.

Finally, to demonstrate reliability or predictive validity of an NR test, one must show that people stay in approximately the same rank order year to year or test to test. This is independent of absolute score, because the entire population can grow in height, knowledge, or skill, as they do in physical stature, and still the individuals would stay in approximately the same position relative to each other. A prime example of that is, of course, that the top third of readers in first grade are likely also to remain in the top third by fourth grade, whether the whole school improves or not in those 3 years.

For CR purposes, the contrasts with the above are striking. The individual's score *is* important in and of itself because it is intended to be a measure of level of knowledge or skill. First, it makes sense to speak of being a novice or an expert only in some domain, so the domain of the skills must be specified explicitly. Test items or performances must therefore be congruent with instructional goals, making those assessments domain referenced (Hively, 1974; Nitko, 1980; Popham, 1978).

Second, for reliability and validity of measurement, we do not want items to fool half the people all the time. Perhaps we want all the students to fail the test before instruction and all of them to pass after instruction—a measure called "instructional sensitivity" (Haladyna & Roid, 1981), but that's the closest we would want items with difficulty of .5. Because effective instruction should help— indeed, require—students to be achieving at 80% correct or higher on tests, then typical NR measures of reliability and validity will be underestimates. A psychometrically appropriate CR assessment is completed via a standard decision table, such as Table 1.1. This is

Table 1.1   Decisions About Mastery

	Test Results	
Level of Competence	*Mastered*	*Did Not Master*
Truly competent	Correct-positive	False-negative
Not competent	False-positive	Correct-negative

because decisions about mastery, like medical diagnoses, fall into one of the following categories (Gentile, 1997, p. 490):

1. A truly competent individual passes the test (a correct-positive decision).

2. A truly competent individual fails the test (a false-negative decision).

3. A truly incompetent individual fails the test (a correct-negative decision).

4. A truly incompetent individual passes the test (a false-positive decision).

This kind of decision table allows the passing standard to be placed wherever it needs to be for the current CR purposes. For example, it might be 70% for initial mastery of multiplication tables, and 85% 2 months later. Changing the passing standard also changes the probability of types of errors: That is, if the standard is too low, we will make more false-positive decisions. How high the standard should be, therefore, depends on how high the stakes are (e.g., Millman, 1989). Given all this and in contrast with NR measures, once these standards are established, each individual's score is directly interpretable as a measure of competence in the domain being tested.

Finally, there are statistical procedures for assessing the reliability and validity of CR assessments, following the logic of Table 1.1 and in parallel with methods of assessing the adequacy of interrater agreements, providing measures such as the percentage of agreements (e.g., Gentile, 1997; Martuza, 1977).

In sum, measurement decisions are fundamentally different for NR and CR purposes, and even if they are correlated (because students who hold the top ranks in class are most likely to pass any given test), it is psychologically different for both teachers and students to conceive of passing a test as a self-actualization rather than as a competition.

Theoretical Bases

Learned Helplessness

Let's return for a moment to the students in Figure 1.2B. If their first experience in learning fractions, say, is unsuccessful, they will forget all or most of it. Next year, they may even claim that they "never had this stuff before," and they will probably believe it. On the second time through, if they are still unsuccessful (which is likely, because teachers usually spend less time reviewing previous material than was spent on initial learning), they will demonstrate little savings and forget again. By the third and fourth exposures to the material, they at least remember they had it before, but may stop trying and explain their lack of motivation with statements such as "I was never very good at math" or "Why do we have to learn this stuff anyway? I'm never going to use it." *Learned helplessness* has set in.

Under laboratory conditions, learned helplessness is developed by first exposing animals or humans to a series of experiences in which failure is inevitable and beyond their control (e.g., Peterson, Maier, & Seligman, 1993; Seligman, 1975). Later, when success is now possible and personally controllable, the victim does not even try. On the emotional level, there is a heightened state of fear, which if prolonged, can easily turn into apathy or depression. On the behavioral/motivational level, there is no perseverance or willingness even for trial-and-error searches (because "Nothing I do ever satisfies these people"). On the cognitive level, there is no discovery of what works, no understanding or organization of an information base, and a long list of defensive excuses or causal attributions, such as "I was never very good at this" and "I could do it if I want to, but school sucks" (the former a primarily female attribution, the latter male; e.g., Dweck & Licht, 1980). It is also more self-protective to adopt a strategy of not trying—or pretending not to try—than to try and not succeed.

Math seems to be a field particularly vulnerable to learned helplessness, because new topics and courses seem to be quite different from previous ones (from multiplication of whole numbers to fractions, arithmetic to algebra to trigonometry, etc.). Even having great success at earlier levels does not immunize against having difficulty on a new topic. Thus even being a "good" student or having 100% success does not guarantee against learned helplessness later, particularly if what students have been good at is memorizing without understanding.

But those primarily at risk for learned helplessness are those who come to school and have not mastered fundamentals (as mentioned earlier). If we teachers cannot diagnose their problems correctly—and early—they are almost destined to fail to master the new tasks. Sadly, to continue the math example, many teachers are not skilled enough themselves to diagnose a child's problems with addition and subtraction as being a deficit in rational counting or one-to-one correspondence. Thus these students comprise the population in Figure 1.2B.

Is there a cure? As in health, prevention is easier than cure. With his learned-helpless dogs, Seligman (1975) literally had to drag them across the barrier to escape electric shock, anywhere from 25 to 200 times, before they once again tried to explore and control their environment. With humans, whose patterns of thought ("I was never very good at this") may reinforce the helpless-behavior patterns, dragging is more figurative than literal. In any case, the cure for helplessness is competence, and only when students are succeeding do feelings of self-efficacy, self-control, and self-esteem begin to follow (see also Bandura, 1977, 1986).

Psychosocial Development

Virtually every theory of human development speaks of the passages from one stage to another as milestones to be achieved, crises to be resolved, or self-worth to be earned. None treat development as a maturational unfolding. Piaget and Inhelder (1969) suggest that children are motivated to move from preconservation to conservation (e.g., that the amount of liquid does not change when poured into a taller, thinner glass) only when they experience a *cognitive conflict* (e.g., their prediction that there is more water in the taller glass is disconfirmed by pouring it back). Vygotsky's (1962, 1978) writings are laced with terms such as *turning point, struggle, leap,* and *rupture.* And central to Erikson's theory (1963, 1968), is the concept of *identity crisis*—a different one for each of his eight stages from infancy through old age.

Of most relevance to the present discussion is Erikson's analysis of the developmental tasks of school age, corresponding roughly from age 6 to puberty. The identity crisis to be resolved is that of *industry* versus *inferiority,* in which children are beginning to formulate their identities by what they can do: "I am what I can learn to make work" (Erikson, 1968, p. 127) or "I am what I learn" (Erikson, 1980, p. 87).

During this age range, the developmental tasks set by our technological society concern verbal and numerical literacy, information-handling skills, and the interpersonal abilities to negotiate these in complex social situations, such as schools. Failure to master these skills results in inferiority, guilt, and lack of self-worth and self-esteem. No amount of well-intended praise for trying—and certainly no amount of providing labels as excuses, such as a specific learning disability—can rectify or compensate for failure at these tasks. Self-worth at this age, readiness for the crises of adolescence, and dreams for the future as an adult—in a word, *identity*—can be achieved only in the old-fashioned way: by *earning* it via competence in these elementary school tasks.

When today's educators say in the various standards that "All children can learn" or in politics that "No child will be left behind," they are recognizing the importance of success at each level of schooling as being preparatory for the next level and for an adult career. We also know, from Erikson's work, that success is even more important than that: It goes to the core of each child's identity. And so we must say to educators, as we say to our children, "If at first you don't succeed, try, try again."

Carroll's Model of School Learning

There are two basic systems of mastery learning (introduced here and discussed in more detail in the Appendix), each derived from different theories but having objectives, a mastery standard, and CR testing in common. The first, Fred Keller's (1968; Keller & Sherman, 1974) Personalized System of Instruction (PSI), is an individually paced system with few large-group lessons. It was developed on a behavioral model in which progress through a curriculum is contingent on successful completion of required and optional assignments (tests, performances, papers, etc.), but this is accomplished by students at their own rates.

The second model, Learning for Mastery (LFM), is a mostly group-based approach, with individualization provided as needed. Like Keller's PSI, it was also published in 1968, by Benjamin Bloom, who derived it from John Carroll's (1963) Model of School Learning. Carroll's model (see also Carroll, 1989) can be succinctly formulated in the following ratio:

$$\text{Amount of Learning} = \frac{\text{Time Actually Spent}}{\text{Time Needed}}$$

That is, what students learn is a function of whether they spend the time they need to learn it.

Contributing to *time spent* are two factors: *opportunity*, defined as the time allowed or scheduled for learning by the teacher, and *perseverance*, which is the time a student is willing or motivated to spend. Contributing to *time needed* are three factors: *quality of instruction*, which includes how well the material is sequenced, presented, and adapted to the learners; *ability to understand instruction*, defined as the extent to which students can comprehend the language of instruction and requirements of the task; and *aptitude*, expressed simply as the time required by an individual to learn some material or skill to some preestablished level.

By Carroll's model, then, we might estimate that Peter and Alicia were likely to need about 3 hours and 1 hour, respectively, to learn how to multiply fractions, based mostly on our experience of teaching them addition and subtraction of fractions by similar methods. If our schedule provides only 2 hours of instruction and practice, however, Peter's learning cannot exceed 2/3 (two thirds of it learned well or more likely, most of it partially learned), while Alicia can attain mastery (and go beyond 2/1). If they both miss 1 of the 2 hours of class (by being physically or cognitively absent), then Alicia may still be able to master the concepts (1/1), but Peter will have barely begun (1/3).

Although it may often appear difficult to quantify these variables, Carroll's model has become far more valuable as a philosophy than as a numerical formula. *Aptitude* had traditionally been defined as an intellectual trait, potential, or capacity; thus Carroll's definition as time needed was radical. It suggested to Bloom (1971, 1981), for example, that for most objectives and standards adopted for schools, all students can learn but they will differ in rates of mastery according to their aptitudes. It furthermore allowed vastly different amounts of time needed by each individual in different domains (e.g., Alicia may have higher aptitude for math than for music). This notion has recently gained further credibility with the popularity of Gardner's (1983, 1993) theory of multiple intelligences.

Whether or not it relates well to other theories, Carroll's view of aptitude has become integral to mastery learning systems, as well as to standards. From phrases such as "All children can learn" to the newly adopted Regents diploma to be required for every high school graduate in New York State, this view is central.

The Brain Base

It is beyond the scope of this book to go into much detail on what has come to be known as "brain-based education," but the popularity of the movement during the last decade requires at least a few comments. Structurally, the brain is usually described as being comprised of the following major parts (e.g., Sousa, 2001):

1. The *brain stem* (also known as the "reptilian brain"), controls the bodily functions that keep us alive, such as heart rate, respiration, digestion, and attention to signals in the environment that may constitute threats.

2. The *limbic system* (also known as "the old mammalian brain") generates emotions and consolidates experiences into memories, thus providing continual interplay between cognitive and emotional processes.

3. The *cerebrum*, or cerebral cortex, is divided into two hemispheres (the so-called right and left brains), which are responsible for speech, thinking, and almost every other kind of act we call cognitive.

4. The *cerebellum* coordinates movements and, likely, their relation to sensations, cognitions, and emotions.

Each of these parts comprises other structures, some of which have unique functions but are often capable of duplicating functions from other parts of the brain. Within each structure are billions of cells, the most central of which (for our purposes) are neurons, or nerve cells, which function to make connections with other neurons. They do this by extending dendrites, or branches, to other neurons and making synapses, or points of connection across which electrical and chemical impulses travel; this shows up as activity in brain-imaging research and diagnosis.

There is much we don't know about these processes, but two apparently supportable generalizations do seem relevant to the current discussion:

1. *Use it or lose it:* Synaptic connections that are repeatedly stimulated proliferate, while others are eliminated or pruned (e.g., Bruer, 1997).

2. *The brain works as a whole:* Contrary to simplistic right brain-left brain conceptions, environmental stimulation activates many parts of the brain, depending on which patterns (in #1) have been established.

In perhaps the first theory of how the brain learns, Donald Hebb (1959) suggested that repeatedly stimulated connections produced *cell assemblies,* which work as neuronal teams to allow for automatic and relatively effortless performances when an important skill is mastered. This occurs, as noted above, not just because of the connections that are formed but also because of those that are pruned. John Bruer (1997) described this developmental phenomenon as follows:

> At birth, both nonhuman and human primate brains contain synapses that connect brain cells into circuits. Neonates have slightly fewer synaptic connections than do adults. However, early in postnatal development, the infant brain begins to form synapses far in excess of adult levels. This process of synaptic proliferation, called synaptogenesis, continues over a period of months that varies among species. This period of synaptic overproduction is followed by a period of synaptic elimination or pruning. This experience-dependent pruning process, which occurs over a period of years, reduces the overall number of synaptic connections to adult, mature levels, usually around the time of sexual maturity for the species. The mature nervous system has fewer synaptic connections than were present during the developmental peak. *It is the pattern, rather than simply the number, of these connections that form the mature brain's neural circuitry and that support normal brain function.* (p. 5; emphasis added)

Thus what is practiced becomes permanent, and only perfect practice makes perfect. Although this argument can and has been made purely from the psychology of learning processes, neural patterns get formed by learning and overlearning, not just from exposure.

Moreover, neural connections are never just cognitive. Environmental stimuli are processed, first, for whether they are life threatening. If so, they set in motion "fight or flight" reflexes. Then they are processed, connected, and conditioned to emotions, such as fear or happiness. Finally, though the total time may be only milliseconds, they are connected to long-term memories and cognitive processes to help interpret what the stimuli mean and what to do about them. Thus, for example, we not only master musical concepts by organizing our knowledge and performing the correct movement but we also associate feelings of love or patriotism, or what have you, to those songs: We play or listen with feelings that are part of those neural patterns. Or, for example, we associate math with threats, we become fearful, and we establish neural patterns supporting learned helplessness.[3]

The Empirical Base

In the third edition of the *Handbook of Research on Teaching,* Michael Dunkin (1986) reviewed the higher education literature and came to the following conclusion about Fred Keller's individualized (PSI) mastery system:

> The single most significant conclusion to be reached from research on innovatory teaching methods in higher education is that the Keller Plan is clearly superior to other methods with which it has been compared. Indeed, the Keller Plan has been so consistently found superior that it must rank as the method with the greatest research support in the history of research on teaching. (p. 759)

Add Bloom's group-based (LFM) approach, and there have been hundreds of studies and dozens of reviews of those studies, including several meta-analyses.[4] These reviewers consistently agree that the following are the active ingredients for the positive cognitive and affective outcomes of those studies:

1. Clear mastery objectives, properly sequenced for transfer of previous knowledge to current and future lessons

2. A preestablished, high passing standard

3. Grading that is criterion referenced, with corrections that encourage and require achievement of those high standards

Effect sizes in these meta-analyses run in the .4 to .6 range; that is, groups taught by mastery methods tend to do about half a standard deviation better than those taught by the traditional methods with which they were compared. We review much of this evidence in other ways in the Appendix, including explanations of meta-analysis and effect size. Of course, not all reviewers agree on the interpretation of those results, especially since effects are larger on criterion-referenced tests directly tied to the instructional domain than they are on standardized, norm-referenced tests. Thus Stallings and Stipek (1986) concluded that the gains are something like placebo or Hawthorne effects:

> Mastery learning advocates no doubt make an important contribution to student learning by convincing teachers that all

children can master the curriculum. Indeed, the achievement gains for children in mastery-based programs may be explained as much by teachers' enhanced expectations, especially for the low-ability students, as by any other aspect of the program. (p. 746)

If this last conclusion were the correct one (to build on points 1-3 above), mastery learning has a fourth active ingredient: *Experience with mastery learning convinces teachers to believe that all children can learn the course objectives.* The standards have the goal of making teachers accountable for their students' academic achievement; therefore raising teachers' expectations so that they provide additional opportunity for their students to learn is no mean accomplishment.

There are other ways, fortunately, of discerning the meaning of mastery learning effects. Return, for example, to the effects on memory of attaining a high degree of original learning (see Section 2, "The Learning/Memory Base"). Among other things, memory should be greater for students who achieve mastery at original learning than for those who do not. This is also true for both fast and slow learners (see "Memory by Fast and Slow Learners" in the Appendix), which is perhaps not too surprising, because fast and slow learners are identified on tasks in the same domain (e.g., learning word lists or poetry). Suppose, however, that we ask how IQ relates to all of this. We already know, for example, that IQ is moderately but significantly correlated with memory. But suppose we randomly assign half the students to have to achieve a preset standard, while the other half (within the same IQ range) are exposed to the same material but do not have to achieve the preset standard. What happens to the correlation between IQ and surprise delayed-retention test scores?

A dissertation study on this very premise was completed recently, under the senior author's direction, by Marianne Baker (1999). The trait of intelligence was measured by the Cognitive Abilities Test (Thorndike & Hagen, 1986), yielding a composite IQ score as well as component scores for verbal, quantitative, and nonverbal IQ. Learning rate, fast versus slow, was measured by the Verbal Learning subtest of the Wide Range Assessment of Memory and Learning Test (WRAML) (Sheslow & Adams, 1990), and memory was measured by the Story Memory subtest on the WRAML. Specifically, for original learning, a short story was read aloud to fourth and fifth graders individually, immediately followed by a free-recall test on specific items

Table 1.2 Correlations Between Intelligence and Memory With and Without Mastery Standards

Intellectual Trait	Memory After Exposure (N = 39)			Memory After Mastery (N = 42)		
	7 days	14 days	28 days	7 days	14 days	28 days
1. Rate of learning	.36*	.43**	.31*	.11	.16	.16
2. Memory ability	.59**	.56**	.61**	.02	.05	−.02
3. Composite IQ	.49**	.59**	.57**	.06	.13	.19
4. Verbal IQ	.44*	.52**	.50**	−.02	.10	.11
5. Quantitative IQ	.42*	.48**	.45**	.11	.09	.15
6. Nonverbal IQ	.39*	.48**	.50**	.05	.16	.23

SOURCE: Adapted from Baker (1999), from Story C results (see endnote 4).
*p < .05, **p < .01

of information as well as comprehension of ideas in the story. For the mastery group, this process was repeated until each student scored between 75% and 90% correct. The nonmastery group heard the story once and did the free-recall test. A week later, both groups were surprised with a written test of memory for the same items. Then students relearned under their respective conditions and finally were tested for retention again after 14 days and 28 days.

Table 1.2 shows the remarkable results regarding intellectual traits and memory.[5] Under nonmastery conditions—that is, a single exposure for original learning, recall after 7 days, a single relearning opportunity, and then recall after 14 and 28 days—the correlations between intellectual traits and recall are all positive and significant. That is, higher-ability students tend to remember more, as society has come to expect.

In stark contrast, imposing a mastery standard of 75% to 90% correct on original learning and then again at relearning renders those standardized intellectual measures nonpredictors of how much is recalled: The correlations hover around zero and are all nonsignificant.

What mastery to a high standard can do, in summary, is virtually bypass the effects of IQ for specified educational objectives. What is recalled about educational lessons is more dependent on how well the material is mastered than on such traits as rate of learning or general intellectual abilities.

Discussion and Conclusions

Critics usually cite three points in opposition to mastery learning:

1. It helps slower students at the expense of the faster students.

2. It is too oriented toward basic knowledge and skills at the expense of creativity and higher levels of thinking.

3. It requires too much work of the teachers.

Let's consider each in light of the principles and theories previously enumerated. That fast learners are bored to tears waiting for slow ones to catch up is far too true of many educational programs, including badly implemented mastery programs. It is not true at all of Keller's (1968) individualized mastery plan, in which students complete course units at their own pace. For group-based mastery schemes, such as Bloom's (1971), it would be true only if mastery were misconceived solely as passing minimum competency tests, with no incentive for students to use their new competencies for higher-level intellectual purposes.

Thus, to counter Criticism #1, the following are needed:[6]

• *A grading system that earns a minimum passing grade—that is, a C or 70 for passing the initial mastery test with at least 75% to 80% correct.* Under the concept of mastery as a beginning rather than as an end state of learning, even a test score of 100% is just the initial phase of learning-forgetting curves. Thus it should earn an entry-level grade. Not passing the mastery test should have a grade of zero or "incomplete" attached to it so that, like driver's tests, initial mastery is conceived as an all-or-nothing affair: Either you get your license, or you do not.

• *A set of enrichment activities that use but go beyond the basic knowledge, skills, and principles required for mastery.* This includes reports on how these principles are applied in real life, creative projects and experiments, further readings or advanced problems to be solved, cooperative investigations or debates, and—most important—tutoring others (we really learn something well when we teach it). Such activities, because they provide overlearning, distributed practice, organization and construction of knowledge, and the like, earn bonus points when adequately completed: Add 5 to 10 points for each project to the minimum pass of 70, or move from C to B for one advanced project and A for two or three such projects.

Under such a grading scheme, the fast learners will no longer be rewarded with the highest course grades simply for beating out their slower peers. And because neither they nor their parents are likely to be satisfied with a minimal pass, they will have adequate incentive to go beyond initial mastery to earn a higher grade.

If enrichment activities as described above are included, then Criticism #2 is also refuted. To apply, analyze, and synthesize—and especially to tutor—concepts that were recently mastered is necessary and required in any sensible mastery scheme, and these are high-level skills indeed. Both fast and slow learners can be encouraged to extend themselves in such a system, whereas too many existing programs, both mastery and nonmastery, get bogged down doing only the basics.[7]

There is some truth in Criticism #3, that mastery learning is more work for teachers. Especially in the beginning, the teacher needs to (a) decide what is absolutely essential to be mastered, (b) create parallel forms of mastery tests, (c) invent activities and scoring keys/ rubrics for mastery of performances and enrichment activities, (d) organize and order units or lessons to facilitate transfer of learning, and (e) publish and be able to defend the grading scheme, and so forth. Once those are complete—and such tasks can be shared with like-minded colleagues—they will also eventually be mastered and become routine. Then the hard work that remains encourages, indeed requires, each student to master the material and go beyond, which requires extra time providing feedback, conducting remediation and testing sessions, and encouraging students to maximize their potential. To us, that doesn't sound like *extra* work; rather, it is *teachers'* work.

Criticism #3 is often phrased in another way: "Teachers have too much material to cover; they simply don't have time for mastery learning." As demonstrated in previous sections, however, without mastery, more time is wasted because (a) there is little or no savings in relearning when the material is encountered again next month or next year, (b) the fast and slow learners grow farther apart because only the former will show savings, and (c) many students lose motivation, become learned helpless, and/or become alienated from school.

In conclusion, the current standards movement is long on rhetoric about every child learning to high standards, even so-called world class standards. Students and educators come to believe such mythology applies to them only when they are succeeding. Standards and how to teach to them are the bread and butter of mastery learning and criterion-referenced assessment, as documented above. The evidence and logic is there, derived both from successful and misconceived implementations. Will we learn from this accumulated evidence, or will we, a generation from now, be speaking of the need for another "new math," or new world-class standards? The following chapters explore these issues in more depth.

Summary

In this chapter, we have provided an overview of mastery learning and the principles on which it is based. Both a philosophy of instruction and a set of ideas for teaching and assessing, mastery learning requires that each student achieve at least minimal curriculum standards, then review and relearn them (in a spiral curriculum) at ever higher levels of thinking and extended applications. To do this requires that students be assessed in a criterion-referenced fashion, that is, without reference to other students but in direct relation to a specified set of instructional objectives and criteria for evaluating how well they have been attained. Teachers must also understand that what is originally learned is typically soon forgotten and therefore overlearning must be built into the curriculum. Fast and slow learners will benefit equally from such programs by spending the time they need to learn, by solving their identity crises, and thereby substituting earned competence for learned helplessness.

Notes

1. The learning/memory research is not explicit on exactly what the threshold for sufficient original learning is. Our estimate of 60% is probably not too far off, and it also has the virtue of being the lowest passing grade for most schools. Thus in practical memory terms, students who have achieved less than 60% correct at original learning will be mostly indistinguishable a few weeks later from students who have never been exposed to the material at all.

2. For example, Bugelski (1979); DeCecco (1968); Hulse, Egeth, & Deese (1980); Travers (1977). For a practical and readable example of the differences between massed and distributed practice in language learning, see Bloom & Shuell (1981).

3. We are fully aware that a controversy exists about whether there is a direct, logical link between a particular educational tactic and basic brain research (e.g., Bruer, 1999, vs. Brandt, 1999). We tend to side with Bruer (1997, 1999), believing that the inferences and applications usually drawn from brain-based research are the same as—and are more parsimoniously derived from—research on cognitive and behavioral processes. That is, the learning/memory curves and helplessness arguments made in the text were originally derived from specific psychological studies. Although recent

technology allows more complete understanding of the brain mechanisms that must necessarily undergird such generalizations, our understanding of the brain's activities vis-à-vis these psychological processes is still in its infancy. With such a caveat in mind, it is nevertheless interesting to speculate on teaching ideas that, in Brandt's (1999) words, may be "used to supplement what we know from other sources" (p. 238). Recent sources that may be useful in that spirit are Sousa (2001), Sprenger (2000), and Sylwester (2000).

4. For example, Anderson (1985); Anderson & Burns (1987); Arlin (1984); Block, Efthim, & Burns, (1989), Gentile (1997); Guskey & Pigott (1988); Kulik & Kulik (1991); Kulik, Kulik, & Bangert-Drowns (1990); Kulik, Kulik, & Cohen (1979); Martinez & Martinez (1992); Stallings & Stipek (1986).

5. Baker (1999) had a number of other conditions, including two different stories, "B" and "C." The results reported here are from Story C, which, unlike Story B (which had an unexpectedly restricted range of scores) provided a clear test of the hypothesis. Because the IQ measures intercorrelated as expected, and other correlations are in the ranges found by others (e.g., for the correlation between initial trials to relearn the correlation in Baker's study was .36, compared with .35 found by Gentile, Voelkl, Mt. Pleasant, & Monaco [1995] and .34 to .55 found by Stroud & Schoer, 1959), there is every reason to expect these correlations to be valid estimates for these analyses.

6. For other variations on these points for grading purposes, see Gentile (1997, pp. 481-489); Gentile & Murnyack (1989); Gentile & Stevens-Haslinger (1983); Gentile & Wainwright (1994).

7. See also Carroll's (1989) refutation of mastery learning as repetitive drill and practice of basics (p. 28), as well as Chapter 4 in this book.

2

Examining
the Standards

Math, Science, Social
Studies, and English Language Arts

This chapter presents the standards developed by national professional organizations of the four major disciplines involved in school curricula: mathematics, science, social studies, and English language arts. In each discipline, we first summarize the goals and scope of the standards, trying very hard to stay within the spirit in which they were intended by the authors. Then we analyze them in some detail to ascertain where and how the intent of those standards overlaps with the philosophy and intent of mastery learning. Finally, we offer several specific suggestions and examples of how implementation of those standards can be improved by including mastery learning procedures. We should note that rather than focusing on state and/or local standards, we have chosen to focus here on national standards to provide a broad treatment of the topic. Furthermore, there is considerable overlap among the national, state, and local standards, with national standards often serving as the foundation for those developed at the state and local levels (see Chapter 3 for a more detailed discussion of this point).

As was perhaps inevitable, each discipline requires that mastery learning be adopted or adapted in somewhat different ways, commensurate with the unique goals and challenges of that discipline. Nevertheless, the fundamental tenets of mastery learning need not be compromised but, we believe, rise to meet those challenges in ways that are not only effective but also help to facilitate the expansion of teachers' instructional repertoires. In the interest of expanding one's repertoire, we urge readers to consider all four of the standards in this chapter, because the unique goals of each discipline seem both complementary to one another and instructive (e.g., inquiry, though stressed in science, is also important in other fields; writing, stressed in English language arts, is likewise important in other fields).

We have already elucidated the theoretical premises and logical bases for mastery learning in Chapter 1. Two additional and related points need particular emphasis in the context of the standards we are about to explore. These are the ideas of "mastery as a beginning" and what it means to go "beyond mastery" to include a wide range of cognitive processes. We turn briefly to each of these.

Mastery as a Beginning

As noted in Chapter 1, it is a common mistake to implement mastery learning as a series of objectives to be checked off when students demonstrate initial achievement of each. This "inoculation theory" of mastery assumes that once we've "had" or mastered an objective, we've finished with it. Clearly, however, this is not how the learning process works. Material initially mastered will be forgotten but can be relearned more quickly (see "Memory by Fast and Slow Learners" in the Appendix). Furthermore, with relearning comes *distributed practice* and *overlearning*, which serves to provide practice for automatizing important skills so that conscious attention can be directed to other things (e.g., comprehension of text is easier when decoding skills are automatized). As part of a well-designed spiral curriculum (Bruner, 1960), such overlearning occurs in new contexts or examples and thus serves as the basis for construction and organization of knowledge, application to new situations or problems, inquiry, and creativity.

To take a simple example we have all experienced, consider driving, in which passing a written and a performance test are the indicators of initial mastery. Given the commonly held belief that meeting a minimum standard marks the end of the learning process, why are we so reluctant to hand our keys over to a newly licensed teenager? The answer, which we all know intuitively, is that reaching that minimum standard is the beginning of the learning process, not the end. In fact, many states have a probationary period for new drivers, during which time any driving infraction results in a loss or suspension of a license. Unlike learning in areas such as grammar or algebra, most students attaining a minimum driving standard don't see obtaining a driver's license as an end, but clearly as a beginning: Now they can begin to drive, which is where their beginning skills and driving judgment will continue to improve and become resistant to forgetting. Other experiences from real life replicate this pattern. For example, when we learn a backhand stroke in tennis or a new chord on the guitar, we do not say "Good, I'm finished with that." Rather, we are now eager to begin to use it in tennis games or in playing more songs. This type of experience will ideally be obtained through students' motivation to continue driving. In fact, if students were not motivated to drive, they would probably forget a great deal of what they were required to learn to obtain their licenses in the first place.

Unfortunately, students are not as motivated to engage in academic subjects as they are driving. Thus it is not surprising (although we as teachers continue to be surprised) that students often forget a great deal of what they have learned or in many cases what we thought they'd learned, when it is often the case that only 20% of students in a typical classroom master the objectives (Bloom, 1986). The remedy for this problem is at least threefold: (a) Require all students to attain initial mastery of the objective; (b) provide enrichment activities for students who attain mastery before the rest of the class, allowing students to revisit the objective through a different learning activity; and (c) continue to revisit the objective at a later point in the curriculum. The first of these is obviously concerned with initial learning. The latter two concern overlearning—practice beyond first mastery of material or skills and additional cognitive processing of the material. Consider any competence you have developed, be it sport, hobby, or academic area, and it is virtually guaranteed that you developed that competence through this process of learning, overlearning to automaticity, and additional cognitive reflections.

Beyond Mastery

Bloom's Taxonomy

It should not be surprising that the *taxonomy of educational objectives* known as the *Bloom taxonomy* is associated with mastery learning, because it is the same Benjamin Bloom who is famous for both. The taxonomy, edited by Bloom, was developed by a committee and published in 1956 to expand teaching and testing beyond the lowest levels of rote learning that were considered to dominate teaching in those days. By 1968, Bloom had launched his version of mastery learning, based on John Carroll's model of school learning (see Bloom, 1971).

Although some might have considered these separate paths in a career, Bloom immediately set out to consider how both of these fields could profitably converge to improve teaching and testing. The result of this work (Bloom, Hastings, & Madaus, 1971) was the *Handbook of Formative and Summative Evaluation of Student Learning*, which, in many ways, was an attempt to do what the current standards do: provide standards at multiple levels of cognitive processing for each of the major subjects taught and at varying grade levels.

Other taxonomies of thinking have since been developed (e.g., Ennis, 1987), including Marzano's (2001) modernization of Bloom's taxonomy (a description follows). However, the Bloom taxonomy is widely known by educators, has only six already familiar major categories, and remains integral to those who trace mastery learning to Bloom's legacy. The Bloom taxonomy identifies six levels of cognitive processing, which progress from the simplest to the most complex. The six levels—knowledge, comprehension, application, analysis, synthesis, and evaluation—are outlined in Table 2.1, with definitions, examples, and the *National Science Education Standards* requiring a given level of processing.

Clearly the *Science Standards,* as well as the other learning standards discussed throughout this text, intend for students to develop the ability to engage in processing at each of the levels of the taxonomy. Similarly, mastery learning applies to each of the levels, because each of the levels identifies skills and information that will serve as prerequisites for future learning.

We should add a caveat for those who are new to this taxonomy: The levels do not represent developmental levels that correspond to a given age or range of ages. In fact, processing at all levels is possible at virtually any age. A common example that demonstrates this quite nicely is based on Edith Lowe's familiar children's story "Goldilocks and the Three Bears." Consider a young child's ability to respond to the following:

- *Knowledge:* Recall the items used by Goldilocks in the Three Bears' house.
- *Comprehension:* Explain why Goldilocks liked the Baby Bear's bed the best.

Table 2.1   Bloom's Taxonomy With Science Examples and
Standards

Level of Processing	Example	Standard
Knowledge: Remember and recall information.	Students can express that animals need air, water, and food; plants require air, water, nutrients, and light.	Students should develop understanding of the characteristics of organisms, including that organisms have basic needs.
Comprehension: Understand the relations between facts or concepts.	Students can explain that the lion, a carnivore, relies on plants because it preys on zebras, which are herbivores.	Students should develop understanding of the characteristics of organisms. All animals depend on plants.
Application: Use information and procedures that are comprehended.	Students keep weather journals, use instruments, and record their observations and measurements.	Students should develop an understanding of changes in earth and sky.
Analysis: Break down an idea into component parts to organize or categorize, compare, and contrast.	By planting seeds in a variety of soil samples, students can compare the effects of different soils on plant growth.	Students should develop an understanding of properties of earth materials
Synthesis: Arrange component parts in some way to form a new, original whole, create new products.	Students design an experiment to determine the effect of various combinations of water and light on the growth of plants and explain the outcome of the experiment.	Students can learn to design investigations and interpret data.

(Continued)

Table 2.1 (Continued)

Level of Processing	Example	Standard
Evaluation: Make judgments regarding the value of information or actions with distinct criteria in mind.	Students can determine the best observations or measurements for determining when to begin planting a spring garden, considering criteria such as ability to withstand a light frost, a colorful garden, etc.	Students can begin to recognize the relationship between explanation and evidence.

- *Application:* Demonstrate what Goldilocks would use if she came into your house.
- *Analysis:* Compare the story to reality. What events could not have happened?
- *Synthesis:* How would the story be different if it was "Goldilocks and the Three Fish"?
- *Evaluation:* Judge whether Goldilocks was bad or good and explain why, using criteria such as following rules, hurting or damaging anyone or anything, and apologizing for mistakes.

Clearly, young children would be able to respond to all or most of these when appropriately questioned, demonstrating that the taxonomy is not developmental. For other examples of objectives at all six levels of the Bloom taxonomy for a single instructional goal, see Gentile (1993, 1997).

Another instructional point concerns sequencing. Nothing in the taxonomy requires that we first teach knowledge, then comprehension, and so forth. Effective teachers often first present a problem or a case (application level) to pique students' interest in understanding a phenomenon or acquiring factual knowledge. Thus a good mastery program does not require endless drill and practice before going on to higher-level or more interesting tasks;

on the contrary, such a drill-and-practice program of minimum competencies on simple tasks is here defined as evidence of a bad mastery learning program.

The Marzano Taxonomy

In a recent attempt to modernize Bloom's taxonomy, Robert Marzano (2001) restructured and reconceptualized Bloom's hierarchy into six different categories. Whereas Bloom's taxonomy was developed as a hierarchy of levels of thinking or levels of processing academic content, Marzano's incorporates those levels of thinking as cognitive processes into a hierarchy of amount of conscious control required. The resulting taxonomy reflects modern conceptions of cognitive and metacognitive processes, as well as their interaction with self-efficacy, perceived self-efficacy, and their motivational and emotional underpinnings. The six levels can be succinctly described as follows:

System	Level	Description
Cognitive	1. Retrieval	Processes of procedural knowledge, recalling or performing but without understanding
	2. Comprehension	Processes of organizing or structuring knowledge, synthesizing and representing it in a rudimentary manner for basic or initial understanding
	3. Analysis	Processes of accessing and examining knowledge for similarities and differences, superordinate and subordinate relations, diagnosis for errors, or from which logical consequences or principles can be inferred

(Continued)

	4. Utilization	Processes of using knowledge from which problems can be posed or solved, investigations can be planned, decisions and applications can be derived
Metacognitive	5. Metacognition	Processes of monitoring whether and how well knowledge is understood, consciously examining the above cognitive processes to see whether they are properly executed and/or reflecting on whether goals are being achieved
Self-system	6. Self	Processes of identifying emotional responses, examining perceptions and motivation, and self-efficacy beliefs in regard to this domain of knowledge

As should be obvious, the taxonomy moves (a) from relatively simple to more complex processing of information or procedures, (b) from less to more consciousness about or control over the processing of knowledge and how to organize or use it, and (c) from less personal involvement or commitment to greater centrality of beliefs and reflection vis-à-vis the individual's self-identity.

The six levels also interact with what Marzano calls the "three domains of knowledge": *information* (vocabulary, details and principles of content); *mental procedures* (recalling, classifying generalizing, metacognitive monitoring, etc.); and *psychomotor procedures* (skills and performances) for each of the six levels. Therefore three possible domains of knowledge exist, for a total of 18 categories, in what Marzano (2001, p. 60) calls a "two-dimensional model."

It is beyond the scope of this text to go into more detail on Marzano's taxonomy, but, like Bloom, he provides many examples of the types of academic tasks that fit into the various categories. Table 2.2 provides a few math examples. In addition, where possible throughout this text, we have classified our examples according to both Bloom's and Marzano's taxonomies.

Table 2.2 Marzano's Taxonomy With Mathematics Example

Level of Processing	Domain of Knowledge	Example
Retrieval	Information	Students know multiplication and division facts (e.g., $6 \times 9 =$ ___ , $54 \div 6 =$ ___).
	Mental procedures	Students know that basic multiplication and division facts are best memorized and practiced regularly.
	Psychomotor procedures	Students can use multiplication and division algorithms (e.g., $38 \times 57 =$ ___ , $54 \div 22 =$ ___).
Comprehension	Information	Students can explain why division of fractions leads to a number larger than either fraction (e.g., by analogy to whole numbers: $3/5 \div 1/8 =$ How many eighths there are in $3/5$, as $6 \div 2 =$ How many 2s are there in 6?).
	Mental procedures	Students know that problems such as division of fractions are better understood when represented visually or through meaningful examples for translation of one to another.
	Psychomotor procedures	Students can both solve a division of fractions problem by the "invert and multiply" algorithm but can also illustrate the problem visually (e.g., see Note 2).
Analysis	Information	Given a case study of another person's solution to a problem, students can diagnose what errors were made and what corrections are needed.

(Continued)

Table 2.2 (Continued)

Level of Processing	Domain of Knowledge	Example
	Mental procedures	Given a case study (as above), students can identify what kind of thinking likely led to the errors (e.g., inadequate prerequisite knowledge, calculation errors, faulty thinking) and what kind of cognitive strategies would have helped.
	Psychomotor procedures	Students can derive generalizations about problem-solving strategies from cases and write them as instructions for beginners.
Utilization	Information	Students can solve as well as pose problems that show the application of a principle or algorithm (e.g., write a word problem for an algebraic expression).
	Mental procedures	Students look for similarities and differences among problems, asking how new information or strategies can help acquire more knowledge or solve problems in other domains.
	Psychomotor procedures	When confronted by a novel problem, students consider commonalities with other problems and estimate what a sensible solution would look like before adopting a strategy or algorithm to use.
Metacognition	Information	Students set goals for achieving objectives in math, including what knowledge or skills they

(Continued)

Table 2.2 (Continued)

Level of Processing	Domain of Knowledge	Example
		already have, when they might need help, and how they will have to allocate time.
	Mental procedures	Students recognize the difference between using a math algorithm and having heuristic strategies (to estimate answers and help them assure their answers and strategies are sensible) to check whether they are achieving their goals.
	Psychomotor procedures	Students perform calculations and apply algorithms but self-assess whether they understand what they are doing and why.
Self-system	Information	Students examine their efficacy in the math they are learning and how central it is to them at the present moment and to potential career options.
	Mental procedures	Students examine the motivation for their behavior (e.g., if they quickly give up on a difficult problem, are they avoiding trying to seem dumb?) or their beliefs about the importance of the math objectives (e.g., "I'm going to be a psychologist and I won't need math").
	Psychomotor procedures	Students can identify emotional or motivational roadblocks to learning and invent ways to overcome them (e.g., by diagnosis of what help is needed to remediate previous misconceptions or bad habits, by better study strategies or by improved perseverance).

Mathematics Standards

Overview

Perhaps the most advanced and comprehensive standards are those developed by the National Council of Teachers of Mathematics (NCTM). Based on what their preface called "a landmark trio of standards documents" (NCTM, 1989, 1991, 1995), the NCTM published *Principles and Standards for School Mathematics* (2000) to be both (a) a culmination of a decade of thinking and debate about math standards and (b) a guide for K-12 decision making for teachers, curriculum developers, administrators, researchers, and policymakers.

This definitive document begins with "a vision for school mathematics," followed in Chapter 2 by six principles the NCTM (2000) considers central to the implementation of standards. These principles cover the topics of equity, curriculum, teaching, learning, assessment, and technology. Chapter 3 then presents an overview of standards for the entire K-12 range in 10 separable but overlapping domains:

- Number and operations
- Problem solving
- Algebra
- Reasoning and proof
- Geometry
- Communications
- Measurement
- Connections
- Data analysis and probability
- Representation

The document's next four chapters reconsider these same topics by grade clusters, as follows: K-2, 3-5, 6-8, and 9-12. The final chapter suggests ways of "working together to achieve the vision."

What is the NCTM (2000) vision of the standards? The second sentence of the preface states that "the recommendations are grounded in the belief that all students should learn important mathematics concepts and processes with understanding" (p. ix). Chapter 1 opens with this image:

> Imagine a classroom, a school, or a school district where all students have access to high-quality, engaging mathematics instruction. There are ambitious expectations for all, with

accommodation for those who need it. Knowledgeable teachers have adequate resources to support their work and are continually growing as professionals. The curriculum is mathematically rich, offering students opportunities to learn important mathematical concepts and procedures with understanding. Technology is an essential component of the environment. Students confidently engage in complex mathematical tasks chosen carefully by teachers. They draw on knowledge from a wide variety of mathematical topics, sometimes approaching the same problem from different mathematical perspectives or representing the mathematics in different ways until they find methods that enable them to make progress. Teachers help students make, refine, and explore conjectures on the basis of evidence and the use of reasoning and proof techniques to confirm or disprove those conjectures. Students are flexible and resourceful problem solvers. Alone or in groups and with access to technology, they work productively and reflectively, with the skilled guidance of their teachers. Orally and in writing, students communicate their ideas and results effectively. They value mathematics and engage actively in learning it. (NCTM, 2000, p. 3)

The authors concede that their envisioned classroom is idealized and ambitious, but then again, it provides the star that we can hitch our wagon to.

Links to Mastery

The NCTM principles and standards are carefully written to avoid the appearance of endorsing any particular teaching method or philosophy. Integral to their principles and suggestions, nevertheless, are the central tenets of mastery learning as we described them in Chapter 1. The following are three examples.

All Children Can and Must Learn

"Excellence in mathematics education requires equity, high expectations, and strong support for all students" (NCTM, 2000, p. 12). The core concern of the equity principle is to combat what the NCTM perceives as the pervasive belief in American society that mathematics is only for the select few. In contrast is the widespread belief in universal language literacy: that all can learn to read and write. In parallel with language literacy, the NCTM wants to create the expectation that all students are capable of learning mathematics. They cite specific studies as "well-documented examples" demonstrating that,

> All children, including those who have been traditionally underserved, can learn mathematics when they have access to high quality instructional programs that support their learning. . . . These examples should become the norm rather than the exception in school mathematics education. (NCTM, 2000, p. 14)

Earlier NCTM (2000, p. 12) argued that equity does not require uniformity of instruction and that "reasonable and appropriate accommodations" can be made to help all students succeed. This statement could be interpreted as a means for NCTM to hedge their bets: that for students who do not succeed in their school's curriculum, teachers can give them a watered-down version. Because that seems so unlike the intent and suggestions in the rest of the *Principles and Standards,* however, we believe that this statement means that different methods, examples, and time allocations can and should be found. Otherwise, adopting standards for learning "important mathematical concepts and processes with understanding" (p. 12) would be a cynical exercise.

No, the NCTM *Principles and Standards* is not a cynical document. It is fully consistent with Bloom's argument that upwards of 90% of students are capable of achieving under mastery learning what only 20% had achieved under traditional instruction and with Carroll's (1963, 1989) famous redefinition of aptitude as *time needed to learn* (on which Bloom based his argument). Carroll's theory, you'll recall, suggests that students will achieve given objectives if they spend the time they need. Or in other terms from Carroll's model, given adequate instruction and opportunity, students will succeed if they persevere, defined as being motivated to spend the time they need.

The NCTM *Principles and Standards* recognizes that doing this requires higher expectations (by teachers as well as students), interesting and relevant instructional materials (for diverse cultural backgrounds), increased use of technology (another important issue of access and equity), and teachers confronting their own beliefs, biases, and pedagogical weaknesses (see Chapter 4 of this text).

Mastery of Prerequisites in a Spiral Curriculum

In the *curriculum principle*, the NCTM states,

> A curriculum is more than a collection of activities: it must be coherent, focused on important mathematics and well articulated across the grades. (NCTM, 2000, p. 14)

Two aspects of this section seem central to our focus. First, the NCTM recognizes that some topics are crucial for mastery, and these can be identified by their interconnectedness with other topics, both preceding and following the curricular plan. Because we do not have time to master everything, teachers need to make decisions about what to teach on the basis of students' prior knowledge and future objectives. An effective curriculum helps teachers articulate those decisions "so that fundamental ideas form an integrated whole" (NCTM, 2000, p. 15).

The second point is that it is not mere exposure to but mastery of these fundamentals that matters:

> Students will reach a certain depth of understanding of the concepts and acquire certain levels of fluency with the procedures by prescribed points in the curriculum, so further instruction can assume and build on this understanding and fluency. (NCTM, 2000, p. 30)

As argued throughout the *Principles and Standards*, especially the teaching and learning principles (NCTM, 2000, pp. 16-21) and the ideas in Chapter 3, developing fluency is not just drill and practice. Rather, it is a balance and connection among "factual knowledge, procedural proficiency, and conceptual understanding" (p. 20). Any one of these without the others is insufficient to produce the fluency sought, namely, the kind of autonomous learners who are not only computationally proficient but also make "smart choices about which tools to use and when" (p. 36).

These ideas suggest three sets of mastery objectives to be achieved in each unit: facts, procedures, and conceptual understandings. To master each means achieving adequate original learning (see Figures 1.1 and 1.2) and then having sufficient distributed practice (overlearning) to be able to use formulas or algorithms, estimate answers, and invent various ways to represent or teach a concept. For example, in teaching 4/5 divided by 3/8 for *fluency,* students need to

---

Example 2.1   Teaching Fractions for Fluency

Under the teaching principle, the NCTM recognizes that students *and* also many teachers have not mastered mathematical ideas to the point of fluency. They suggest that teachers need to know "that fractions can be understood as parts of a whole, the quotient of two integers, or a number on a line" (p. 17). Indeed mathematics teachers need to know this because their students cannot be fluent in fractions without learning it. Can you do it?

Item 1: Demonstrate at least the following ways to represent (or teach) the fraction 3/8:

1. As a portion of a whole
2. As a quotient
3. As a point on a number line
4. In some other way of your invention

Item 2: Demonstrate in at least two ways 4/5 divided by 3/8 equals 2.13. See Notes 1 and 2 for suggested ways to solve these problems.

---

know (a) how to multiply and divide numbers to the point of automaticity, (b) the algorithmic and computational procedure of inverting the divisor and why that is necessary, and (c) how to represent their understanding that division of fractions leads to a larger number than the fraction (see Example 2.1, item 2).

Mastery of the unit, then, means being able to do at least all of those processes to some reasonably high standard, say 80% of the problems accurately solved, demonstrated, and represented, in more than one way. Such mastery demonstrates that the student is ready for more advanced analyses, transferring or applying such knowledge to other domains, or other extra-credit work (inventing their own problems or solutions). This is in keeping with mastery as the beginning level of the competence on the road toward expertise (as described in our Chapter 1).

Assessment and Feedback

"Assessment should support the learning of important mathematics and furnish useful information to both teachers and students"

(NCTM, 2000, p. 22). So states the *assessment principle,* which (a) is criterion referenced (tied directly to the instructional objectives and how well each student is doing in regard to them), (b) provides feedback (that is, specific information on what was done correctly, what is incorrect, and how to improve), and (c) is formative rather than summative (because it is part of monitoring students' progress during instruction). In addition to the above, the NCTM hopes to expand teachers' assessment techniques to go beyond timed paper-and-pencil objective tests to more extended constructed responses, including reflective journals and portfolios, as well as performance tests and other demonstrations.

Using Mastery Learning to Implement the NCTM Standards

Consider the following two statements:

• Mathematics comprises different topical strands, such as algebra and geometry, but the strands are highly interconnected. The interconnections should be displayed prominently in the curriculum and in instructional materials and lessons. A coherent curriculum effectively organizes and integrates important mathematical ideas so that students can see how the ideas build on, or connect with, other ideas, thus enabling them to develop new understandings and skills (NCTM, 2000, p. 15).

• The standards for grades 6-8 include a significant emphasis on algebra along with much more geometry than has normally been offered in the middle grades, and call for the integration of these two areas. The standards for grades 9-12, *assuming that the strong foundation in algebra will be in place by the end of the eighth grade,* describes an ambitious program in algebra, geometry, and data analysis and statistics and also call for integration and connections among these ideas (NCTM, 2000, pp. 37-38; emphasis added).

In these two quotations, we can see how the NCTM *Principles and Standards* depend on two fundamentals of instructional theory, one rather explicit, one implicit. The explicit fundamental is the spiral curriculum (e.g., Bruner, 1960), in which central ideas continue to be revisited with new applications and in greater complexity in an elegant synergy of developmental readiness and instructional opportunities. The implicit fundamental is the issue of transfer, "the ability to use previously learned skills or knowledges in settings or on problems different from the original learning, including the capacity to distinguish when and where those learnings are appropriate" (Gentile, 2000b, p. 13).

Unfortunately, this *Encyclopedia of Psychology* entry goes on to say, a century of research and theorizing does not allow for unbridled enthusiasm about how much transfer is likely (Gentile, 2000b). The reasons are that transfer assumes original mastery of the material and adequate recall of it. But then transfer goes beyond those prerequisites to overcome perceptual sets, biases, or interfering beliefs (such as learned helplessness) to invent creative solutions to novel problems or previously unencountered situations. Transfer, in other words, cannot occur without adequate initial mastery and memory and does not automatically occur even with them. Transfer requires establishing the proper instructional experiences. Gentile's (2000b, p. 15) advice follows; it is based on the entire span of transfer research (formal discipline to identical elements to gestalt to interference theory to situational cognition):

- Learners must develop a rich knowledge base and master basic skills to near automaticity.
- Learners must practice multiple methods and strategies to avoid a "one best way" mentality or perceptual set.
- Prior relevant knowledge must be activated in the target situation.
- Learners must be challenged to identify underlying principles and to find how seemingly diverse problems or tasks resemble one another.
- Learners must learn comprehension monitoring and other metacognitive strategies.
- Learners need to negotiate the above in a social context, in which ideas and explanations provide "cognitive conflicts" or "teachable moments" to motivate continual reorganization of their knowledge and skills, as well as improved metacognitive strategies.
- Curricula need to be sequenced so that each new unit reinforces, reviews, and incorporates what was learned in previous units and anticipates subsequent units.
- If situations can be transferred, individual learnings that are contextualized to those situations may follow.

The NCTM aims to promote all of these things, making the *Principles and Standards* entirely consistent with current learning and cognition theory. But have no illusions about the difficulty of the task: Ideas can be built on or connect with other ideas only if they are mastered to a high level, what the *Principles and Standards* called fluency (as cited previously). We cannot merely cover ideas the first time and pass students on in the hope that the spiral curriculum will remediate their insufficiencies later.

In this way, mastery learning is integral to the successful implementation of the NCTM standards. We see two ways to bring mastery learning to the party: (a) by monitoring students' progress during instruction, complemented with a supportive grading scheme (see Chapter 4) and (b) by pretests on prerequisites for each new unit or topic. Each is examined in detail below.

Curriculum-Embedded Assessment and Grading

For the first use of mastery, it is necessary to identify the required mastery objectives, perhaps in two areas (as noted above): computational proficiency and conceptual understanding. Then, similar to a driver's test in which you must know both the rules of the road (as assessed on a multiple-choice test) and how to drive (as assessed by performance), the lowest passing grade is earned by demonstrating competence in each area independently. For the fractions illustrations (Example 2.1), students might have to be able to demonstrate the following to achieve the lowest passing grade (*S* or *C* or 75):

- *Computational proficiency:* finding least common denominators, multiplying and dividing integers, reducing fractions, following multiplication and division algorithms, accuracy to the hundredth place on 9 of 10 problems using a calculator, and so on. This can be assessed by short answer, multiple choice, oral recitation, and so on.

- *Conceptual understanding:* demonstrating three or more ways to represent fractions or two ways to show that division of fractions leads to a larger amount than either fraction. This can be assessed by short essays, drawings, a written report on how to teach this procedure to a beginner, actual tutoring, and/or creation of some problems to use with fellow students. See Example 2.2 for other ideas for grading.

Example 2.2   Rubric for Grading Computational Proficiency
and Conceptual Understanding

The following are two basic grading schemes, one based on
letters and the other numerical, designed to motivate students to
achieve mastery in both computation and conceptual understanding of fractions:

Letter Grade	Numerical Grade	Interpretation of Grades
A (A– to A+)	95 (90-100)	Met the standards for B (or 85) *and* demonstrated advanced proficiency in computation (via automaticity and relatively errorless skills) and conceptual understanding and transfer of skills (via tutoring others, application, projects, written reports, or reflective thinking in a portfolio)
B (B– to B+)	85 (80-89)	Met the standards for C (or 75) *and* demonstrated ability to generate more than one way to solve problems, showed initiative in ability to transfer skills to other problems and/or tutor others, and habitual high levels of computational accuracy
C (C– to C+)	75 (70-79)	Passed required tests and exercises, thus demonstrating computational competency (e.g., at least 80% accuracy on paper-and-pencil tests or in oral recitations) *and* minimal acceptability in conceptual understanding (e.g., can demonstrate at least two ways to represent a fraction or why we need "to invert and multiply" when dividing fractions)

D (D– to D+)	65 (60-69)	Might be able to pass state minimum competency tests, but (1) demonstrates little understanding or ability to transfer knowledge; and/or (2) is not consistently able to compute accurately; *or* does (1) or (2) but not both. Thus has not yet achieved mastery
F	50	Unlikely to pass state competency tests and thus has not mastered either basic computation or conceptual understanding

Mastery as a Pretest

To be prepared for any unit assumes prior knowledge and skills. The previous examples of fractions and division of fractions, for instance, assume fluency with integers and addition and subtraction of fractions. Is it not, therefore, a reasonable procedure to be required to demonstrate proficiency prior to beginning the next unit? Such a procedure is already in widespread use to place students in many high school and college classes, especially in math and language.

At the beginning of a new unit, the teacher announces that first, "We have to make sure some important prerequisite knowledges and skills are fresh in our memories." Thus students practice and prepare (through homework, class exercises, etc.) for a test before embarking on the new material. This preparation (a) activates prior knowledge as an anticipatory set (e.g., Hunter, 1994) or advance organizer (e.g., Ausubel, 1960), (b) allows the teacher to discover any misconceptions that students may harbor before making unwarranted assumptions, and (c) reminds students of the connectedness of the curriculum. This last point seems to us to be especially critical for getting students to trust that the material they are learning now does matter: It shows their progress over earlier learning, and it *will be revisited* later in more complex ways.

Having considered the national math standards, how they share commonalities with mastery, and how mastery can be used to help students meet these and other mathematical standards, we now turn our attention to the national science standards to examine them in much the same manner.

Science Standards

Overview

In 1996, the National Research Council (NRC) responded to a perceived national "goal that all students should achieve scientific literacy" (p. ix). By publishing *National Science Education Standards,* a consortium representing the National Academy of Sciences, the National Academy of Engineering, and the Institute of Medicine, the NRC has a mandate for furthering knowledge and advising the federal government on matters of science. In this case, they developed their standards as a call to action to the public in general and to educators in particular.

> The intent of the Standards can be expressed in a single phrase: Science standards for all students. The phrase embodies both excellence and equity. The Standards apply to all students regardless of age, gender, cultural or ethnic background, disabilities, aspirations, or interest and maturation in science. Different students will activate understanding in different ways and different students will achieve different degrees of depth and breadth of understanding depending on interest, ability, and context. But all students can develop the knowledge and skills described in the Standards even as some students go well beyond these levels. (NRC, 1996, p. 2)

The 1996 *Science Standards* were the culmination of more than a decade of concern about education inaugurated by the publication of *A Nation at Risk* (National Commission on Excellence in Education, 1983). The standards' lineage also includes two publications by the American Association for the Advancement of Science (AAAS; 1989, 1993), as well as reports by the National Science Teachers Association and the NCTM standards documents (mentioned in the section on mathematics standards). These ideas evolved, with considerable review and consensus by the broad range of scientists and educators, into the current standards.

Following an overview, the *Science Standards* are guided by four principles:

- Science is for all students.
- Learning science is an active process.

- School science reflects the intellectual and cultural traditions that characterize the practice of contemporary science.
- Improving science education is part of systemic education reform (NRC, 1996, pp. 20-21).

The actual standards themselves are defined as criteria to judge the quality of (a) teachers and teaching, (b) professional development for teachers, (c) assessments, (d) content and curriculum, (e) school science programs, and (f) the systemic context in which school science programs operate (including political, fiscal, and higher education programs). Within each of the chapters devoted to these topics, there are content standards with particularly exemplary ideas for teaching various scientific concepts at grade levels K-4, 5-8, and 9-12.

Links to Mastery

Because the *Science Standards* are meant to be applicable to policy issues and continuing professional development of teachers as well as to classroom instruction, many issues discussed are not directly related to students' learning. Indeed, concern seems to be more oriented toward documenting the inferences about assessment outcomes than guaranteeing any given outcome. For example, Assessment Standard B, which gives equal weight to assessing student achievement and opportunity, is explained as follows:

> Students cannot be held accountable for achievement unless they are given adequate opportunity to learn science. Therefore, achievement and opportunity to learn science must be assessed equally. (NRC, 1996, p. 83)

Although this may be true enough to help policymakers explain results, it seems too willing to excuse inadequate achievement and thus may be counterproductive to a mastery philosophy. More mastery-friendly interpretations are also possible, and we turn to examples of those next.

"Hands-On, Minds-On"

One of the frustrations many parents feel arises when a child, in attempting to put away homework to do a more preferred activity, dismisses further attention to the task with "But Mom, we don't

have to learn it; we just have to do it." The *Science Standards* are
dedicated to stamping out that attitude and replacing it with developing students' responsibility for their own learning via the skills
of inquiry. That, in turn, requires active and extended investigation,
reflection, and debate on problems of perceived relevance to the
students.

"Inquiry into authentic questions, generated from student experiences, is the central strategy for teaching science" (NRC, 1996, p. 31).
Inquiry is described as follows:

> Students at all grade levels and in every domain of science
> should have the opportunity to use science inquiry and
> develop the ability to think and act in ways associated with
> inquiry, including asking questions, planning and conducting
> investigations, using appropriate tools and techniques to
> gather data, thinking critically and logically about relation-
> ships between evidence and explanations, constructing and
> analyzing alternative explanations, and communicating scien-
> tific arguments. (NRC, 1996, p. 105)

The content standards are explicit in providing less emphasis on
vocabulary, facts, and information in favor of understanding and
integrating scientific content (e.g., NRC, 1996, p. 113). Likewise, one-
class experiments designed to obtain answers or replicate established
findings are de-emphasized in favor of extended investigations that
generate questions and end in logical argument and explanation.
Because these thinking processes are to be "aligned with students'
ages and stages of development" (NRC, 1996, p. 110) and because one
cannot do everything at once, the standards argue, "Students will
engage in selected aspects of inquiry as they learn the scientific way
of knowing the natural world, but they also should develop the
capacity to conduct complete inquiries" (NRC, 1996, p. 23).

To tease out what prerequisites might be considered necessary by
the *Science Standards*, it is necessary to consider the same topic at two
grade levels. Compare Content Standard B in Physical Science on
properties of objects and materials at the K-4 (NRC, 1996, pp. 123-
126) and 5-8 grade levels (NRC, 1996, p. 149). In the early years,
students learn to sort objects in terms of properties such as color, tex-
ture, or hardness and to distinguish between an object and the substances of which it is composed. By the middle school, those skills
must be mastered in order to focus on identifying and measuring
the properties of pure substances of which objects are composed

(e.g. boiling points, solubility, and chemical reactions with other substances).

Similar arguments are made for the study of motions and forces in physics, characteristics of organisms in life sciences, astronomical events in earth and space science, and so forth. Unfortunately, that is as prescriptive as the *Science Standards* get. There are no specific suggestions for exactly what needs to be understood correctly or what misconceptions need to be overcome as a prerequisite to understanding subsequent lessons. Mastery learning could clearly help here, as suggested under mastery as a "pretest" (see the last section, under "Math Standards").

Probably the most influential slogan to arise from the *Science Standards* is that learners must have experiences that are both "hands-on and minds-on." Like all good slogans, this one can rally the troops around a new goal, in this case, to increase the probability of higher-level thinking and inquiry processes replacing rote recall of facts and procedures as the major process of science classes. But thinking is not done in the abstract: Some threshold of knowledge must be achieved in order to have something to think about. Thus there is a delicate balance to be achieved between knowledge and inquiry skills, each of which could benefit by establishing clear criteria for mastery. The *Science Standards* provide an outline for this, but as always, the devil is in the details, and their own examples illustrate the problem (see Example 2.3).

Assessment and Learning

In this new view, assessment and learning are two sides of the same coin. The methods used to collect educational data define in measurable terms what teachers should teach and what students should learn. And when students engage in an assessment exercise, they should learn from it.

This view of assessment places greater confidence in the results of assessment procedures that sample an assortment of variables using diverse data-collection methods rather than the more traditional sampling of one variable by a single method. Thus all aspects of science achievement ability to inquire, scientific understanding of the natural world, and understanding the nature and utility of science are measured using multiple methods such as performances and portfolios, as well as conventional paper-and-pencil tests. (NRC, 1996, p. 76)

Example 2.3   Density: Inquiring Minds Want to Know

The Lessons

In the exemplary illustration for grades 5-8 entitled "Funny Water," the *Science Standards* (NRC, 1996) introduces us to a sequence of lessons by Mr. B. on the difficult concept of density. He wanted his students to do the following:

> Think about the properties of substances as a foundation for the atomic theories they would gradually come to understand in high school. He knew that the students had some vocabulary and some notions of atomicity but were likely not to have any understanding of the evidence of the particular nature of matter or arguments that support that understanding.
>
> He knew that the students who had been in the district elementary schools had already done some work with liquids and that all students brought experience and knowledge from their daily lives. (NRC, 1996, p. 150)

> To begin, he demonstrated the separation of liquids in cylinders (colored water, liquid detergent, syrup, various oils, and methanol) to pique their interest, asking students to think about what they saw. A lively discussion ensued, which he followed up the in next few class periods with small group investigations into these liquid layers, and then with objects (paper clips, rubber bands, wood blocks, chips off the same block, etc.) floating in such liquids. After these experiences, students were to write their ideas in their notebooks. Later, volunteers read from their notebooks. Many students were apparently still struggling with the concept, though they some had reasonably good explanations. Mr. B. then arranged further tests of the hypotheses students were still entertaining. Finally, to close this sequence of lessons, Mr. B. summed up and then assigned them, for homework, (a) to come up with explanations for all that they observed and (b) to find "examples of these phenomena in their daily lives" (NRC, 1996, p. 153).

A Critique

There is much to applaud in this illustration. Among the note-worthy features are the well-planned demonstrations, the use of questions that invite higher level thinking, the apparent ease with which Mr. B. can make transitions from lecture/demonstration mode to various kinds of small groups and large discussions, and the congruence between assignments and objectives.

From a mastery learning point of view, however, the following problems at the very least need to be addressed:

Concerning students' prior knowledge, Mr. B. assumes that they "had some vocabulary and notions" and that they had some experience with liquids. But even if they had, this is no guarantee that they will remember them. It would be better to decide what prerequisites were needed and directly teach or design an activity designed to reinforce the vocabulary and procedures that would be useful in the new lessons.

Concerning inquiry, Mr. B.'s students had no practice whatsoever. In contradiction to the NRC's minimum requirements for inquiry, it was the teacher, Mr. B., who designed all the experiments and demonstrations. All that the students did was invent explanations and find applications, and it is not clear what was to be done with those (since the next lesson after the homework assignment was to be on boiling points).

Concerning understanding, not all students had equal opportunity. For example, when disagreements arose during the initial demonstrations, "Mr. B. suggested that interested students come back during their lunch time to try to resolve these disagreements" (NRC, 1996, p. 151).

Concerning assessment and standards, there are several problems. First, Mr. B. relies mostly on students writing brief explanations in their notebooks, both in class and for homework. How he will grade them is not specified. We will give him the benefit of the doubt that he may have useful rubrics for the homework assignments at least, but in any case, he is using only one way to assess his students' understanding during the lesson.

Second, his students wrote explanations in their notebooks after the initial demonstration, along with the instruction, "There are no right answers, and silence is OK. You need to think" (NRC, 1996, p. 150). Are there really no right answers? Nothing to be mastered here? In addition, does writing a nonsupportable explanation in one's notebook make it compete for memory space when a better explanation becomes available later? But even if not, wouldn't it be better to require students to reflect on their early explanations in light of subsequent discoveries to demonstrate their own growth (as in a portfolio)?

Finally, although Mr. B. required explanations and applications, he did not require sustained and logical arguments.

Concerning grading, it is not at all clear that Mr. B. motivated many of his students to want to learn about density (except for the interested students at lunch). A mastery grading scheme with clear criteria for passing and going beyond could help (as in Example 2.4).

In sum, although Mr. B.'s sequence of lessons has some good ideas in them, it is naive to think that students learned much from these lessons, either facts or inquiry skills. For the latter, as the standards themselves proclaim, the students would have needed to design investigations, construct and analyze alternative hypotheses, and so on.

This clear philosophy formed the basis for our critique of Mr. B.'s density lessons in Example 2.3, which shows, ironically, that despite the NRC's good intentions, it is easier to preach good assessment than to develop lessons that practice it.

In addition, this "new view" (as they call it) can be at least traced to Dewey (1933), who wrote,

We should ridicule a merchant who said he had sold a great many goods although no one had bought any. But perhaps there are teachers who think they have done a good day's teaching irrespective of what pupils have learned. There is the same exact equation between teaching and learning that there is between buying and selling. (pp. 35-36)

In all the assessment literature, the only approach that consistently implemented this Dewey-eyed idea has been mastery learning, with its emphasis on criterion-referenced measurement to assure that each child learns the crucial objectives (and is measured independently of the rest of the students). Compare the basics of mastery learning with these science assessment standards (NRC, 1996):

- "Assessments must be consistent with the decisions they are designed to inform" (p. 78). This is further elaborated as assessments must be "deliberately designed" with "explicitly stated purposes" showing a clear "relationship between the decisions and the data," as well as being "internally consistent" (p. 78).

- "Achievement and opportunity to learn science must be assessed," further elaborated to say that achievement data should focus "on the science content that is most important for students to learn" and "the science all students will come to understand" (p. 79).

Although the *Science Standards* are trying to use language that avoids endorsing specific teaching techniques (e.g., NRC, 1996, p. 23) or theories, they are clearly endorsing a criterion-referenced approach to assessment, with multiple methods of assessing, and therefore teaching each student on important scientific methods of reasoning and organizing knowledge to an acceptable level (or passing standard). Mastery advocates could not have stated it any better.

The *Science Standards* go on to describe the differences between classroom assessments and district, state, or national assessments. The former tend to be more formative (i.e., during learning), to be directly tied to the curriculum, to involve students and teachers and provide timely feedback, and to be lower stakes (i.e., they may be a component of a grade for a unit, but they are not determinative of graduation). The latter tend to be summative (i.e., after learning is complete), to be indirectly tied to the curriculum, to exclude students (and their teachers), to provide no feedback (only a score often in norm-referenced terms), to be high stakes (i.e., determinative of graduation), and to provide data useful mostly to administrators or the public. Mastery learning, of course, occurs at the classroom level.

The final sections of the assessment standards (NRC, 1996, pp. 91-100) provide useful ideas on developing rubrics for scoring students' performances or reasoning similar to that in Example 2.4 (without the grades). Examples are given of "the performance of a scientifically literate adult" and excellent and satisfactory student performances. These are worth pondering at length, because reliability and validity of scoring performances and reasoning requires explicit rubrics in each domain or topic being assessed (e.g., Gentile, 2000a). This is, without a doubt, one of the most difficult tasks teachers face.

Example 2.4   Rubric for Grading Understanding of Density

The following are two basic grading schemes, one based on letters and the other numerical, designed to motivate students to achieve mastery in understanding the concept of density and applying inquiry skills to it.

Letter Grade	Numerical Grade	Interpretation of Grades
A (A– to A+)	95 (90-100)	Met the standards for B (or 85) *and* demonstrated advanced understanding or application of the concept, including the ability to design experiments to test at least two alternative explanations for a research question, with a logical explanation.
B (B– to B+)	85 (80-89)	Met the standards for C (or 75) *and* generated ideas for applying or teaching the concept of density, including logical approaches to the relationship between evidence and explanations.
C (C– to C+)	75 (70-79)	Passed required tests on the meaning of density and how it differs from other concepts such as weight (by scoring at least 80% on paper-and-pencil-tests) and can demonstrate/replicate a classic experiment to gather evidence on density of several substances.
D (D– to D+)	65 (60-69)	Might be able to pass state minimum competency tests, but (1) demonstrates little understanding of the concept of density and its applications; and/or (2) is not able to demonstrate/replicate a classic experiment to gather evidence; or does (1) or (2) but not both. Thus has not yet achieved mastery.

F	50	Unlikely to pass state competency tests and thus has not mastered the concept of density nor adequate inquiry skills for this grade level.

Using Mastery to Implement the NRC Standards

Our critique of Mr. B.'s lessons in Example 2.3 provides the bases on which mastery learning can increase the probability of success of the *Science Standards*. Because the standards suggest that both student achievement and opportunity to learn be assessed, they have inadvertently allied themselves to Carroll's model of school learning (see Chapter 1 of this text), in which a student's learning is a function of time spent divided by time needed (aptitude and other variables). Time spent, you'll recall, is comprised of two variables: *opportunity* (time allowed) and *perseverance* (the time the student actually spends). From this, one can deduce that if a student is provided with 2 hours of instruction on a topic but is absent or has an attention lapse such that he or she spends only 1 of those hours on task, then it is the lower of those numbers (1) that serves as the numerator in Carroll's equation. For a high-aptitude student who needs only 1 hour to learn the material, 1/1 predicts 100% achievement. For a low-aptitude student, however, who might need 3 hours, Carroll's model predicts 1/3, or 33% achievement.

As noted in Chapter 1, providing numerical estimates of a student's performance is a noteworthy feature of Carroll's model, but its most important contribution is to explicate testable relationships using these variables. The *Science Standards* could benefit from this because as noted above, it tends to treat opportunity as an excuse for a student's, teacher's, or district's inability to achieve the goals of the curriculum. Furthermore, the standards need to be clear that the bottom line is not whether the teachers provide opportunity, but whether they entice their students to persevere to take advantage of the opportunity.

Mastery learning is directly concerned with all of the following issues raised by the *Science Standards:*

- Identify the objectives.
- Assess what the students already know or can do regarding those objectives.
- Invent exercises so that the students may not only acquire knowledge but also organize and use that knowledge to acquire more knowledge, solve problems, and test hypotheses.
- Assess in ways consistent with the above to ensure that all students receive feedback and are at least minimally competent vis-à-vis those objectives.
- Devise exercises and follow-up assessments to remediate students who at first fail to achieve minimum acceptable performances.
- Create a grading system and exercises designed to entice students to go beyond competence and work toward true expertise (via peer tutoring, advanced projects, etc.).

The standards emphasize that this can all be best accomplished by multiple methods of teaching and assessment. This is consistent with our points made about transfer (see our recommendations on "Using Mastery to Implement the NCTM Standards") as well as with our critique about what was needed in Mr. B.'s assessments of density (Example 2.3).

Social Studies Standards

Overview

> Social studies is the integrated study of the social sciences and humanities to promote civic competence. Within the school program, social studies provides coordinated, systematic study drawing upon such disciplines as anthropology, archaeology, economics, geography, history, law, philosophy, political science, psychology, religion, and sociology, as well as appropriate content from the humanities, mathematics and natural sciences. The primary purpose of social studies is to help young people develop the ability to make informed and reasoned decisions for the public good as citizens of a culturally diverse, democratic society in an interdependent world. (National Council for the Social Studies, 1994, p. 3)

This was the definition adopted in 1992 by the National Council for the Social Studies (NCSS) when they initiated a task force to develop standards to guide curriculum planning, teaching, and assessment for American schools, K-12. Because the social studies draw from so many academic disciplines without necessarily studying each discipline per se, coordinating and integrating many ways of understanding a problem is a daunting task. No individual teacher can claim expertise in more than one or two of these disciplines, and yet a comprehensive comparative study of cultures, for example, may need to draw on all of them.

Because of this multidisciplinary complexity, the NCSS adopted 10 thematic strands into which specific disciplinary perspectives can be integrated, but which are holistic topics to be explored in greater breadth and depth in a well-planned spiral curriculum. These themes are identified as follows (NCSS, 1994, pp. x-xii):

- Culture: commonalities and differences
- Time, continuity and change: historical roots for the present and future
- People, places, and environments: geographical contexts
- Individual development and identity: psychosocial and cultural influences
- Individuals, groups, and institutions: sociocultural, political, and religious influences
- Power, authority, and governance: political, legal, and historical roots and trends
- Production, distribution, and consumption: economics and politics
- Science, technology, and society: cultural and ethical contexts
- Global connections: historical roots and current political and economic interdependencies
- Civic ideas and practices: the balance between citizen rights and responsibilities

The NCSS bases the above themes on the mandates of U.S. democracy, as the following introductory anecdote and commentary illustrates:

As Ben Franklin was leaving the constitutional convention one afternoon in September 1787, a young woman approached him and asked, "Well, Dr. Franklin, what have you given us?"

"A republic, if you can keep it," was his reply.

Keeping the republic requires that United States citizens labor
vigilantly to ensure that this form of government continues to
extend the blessings of liberty to all its citizens. (NCSS, 1994,
p. xix)

Students are not just expected to learn about and from history
or to respect diversity of religion or culture. Most important, they are
to "assume the office of citizen" (NCSS, 1994, p. 3) as the founding
fathers intended: Vote intelligently; be actively committed to our
values and, for example, defend someone's right to say or believe something that is unpopular; and make informed and multidimensional
decisions when two or more values come into conflict (e.g., majority
rule vs. religious freedom; NCSS, 1994, p. xv). Students must not
learn just the content or their own rights; they must learn to consider
"the common good" and to be sufficiently analytical to "understand
that their self-interest is dependent upon the well-being of others in
the community" (NCSS, 1994, p. 6).

Links to Mastery

The above goals are a tall order indeed, especially for individuals
or groups whose eagerness for defending unpopular causes varies
inversely with the distance from their own skin. Critical thinking, in
other words, is fine as long as it isn't critical of "my beliefs." Multiple
perspectives are fine so long as they don't undermine "my valued
truths." That this might not be easy is recognized by the NCSS (1994;
see also pp. 166-67):

Teachers need both the freedom and the fortitude to address
the real social world (not simply an idealized version) and to
engage students in critical thinking about controversial topics.
As they work to help students come to grips with social
issues, teachers have both a responsibility to avoid inappropriate promotion of their personal views and a right to expect
administrative and community support for their citizen education efforts. (p. 162)

Mastery learning is integral to the NCSS goals and can help in at
least the three ways discussed next.

Teaching Critical Thinking via Controversial Topics

One of the precepts of the NCSS standards is that instruction
should be value based and should not shy away from disturbing or

controversial aspects of real-life treatments of the topic. In this section, they conclude as follows:

> Powerful social studies teaching encourages recognition of opposing points of view, respect for well-supported positions, sensitivity to cultural similarities and differences, and a commitment to social responsibility and action. It recognizes the reality and persistence of tensions but promotes positive human relationships built on understanding, commitment to the common good and willingness to compromise and search for common good. (NCSS, 1994, p. 167)

Fundamental to respect for others' points of view is understanding them. At the most basic level, this requires being able to defend the opposing view yourself and/or provide the arguments the way opposing lawyers would. Richard Paul (1987) provides useful instructional suggestions for this in the method he calls *dialogical thinking*. Such thinking is also central to the procedures used in conflict resolution or counseling, in which the initial steps are to list and then restate the other party's perception of the problem (e.g., Johnson & Johnson, 1991, 1995; Meier & Davis, 1996).

This immediately suggests an avenue of assessment: Students must demonstrate their comprehension of each position on the controversial topic, mastery of which could be considered as a prerequisite to searches for common solutions. Often, however, even comprehension of another's position is impossible without fundamental background knowledge of the person's culture, religion, or history vis-à-vis the controversial topic. By requiring students to pass a criterion-referenced test on such fundamentals prior to or as part of the learning-to-respect-opposing-viewpoints exercises, subsequent critical thinking exercises will be better informed with relevant facts. An example of how to do this with the NCSS's own example of prayer in the schools is provided in the next section, "Using Mastery Learning to Implement the NCSS Standards," "A High School Lesson on Cultural Diversity."

Opportunity for All

Consistent with the mathematics and science standards discussed in this chapter, the NCSS (1994) expects that *"All students should have access to the full richness of the social studies curriculum"* (p. 162, italics in original). Not just the gifted or students in a college track, but even at-risk or special education students as well as those in vocational or other tracks should be included in an "ongoing engagement in thinking about social and civic problems and policy issues" (p. 162).

Such universal opportunity is to be implemented by teaching and learning exercises designed to be "meaningful, integrative, value-based, challenging, and active" (see NCSS, 1994, pp. 162-170). This can be achieved only through sustained inquiry at multiple levels of thinking, from gathering important facts to critical thinking, about issues and applications that are meaningful to the students. The NCSS (1994) elaborates on meaningfulness as depth, rather than breadth, of coverage on the most representative or inspiring cases. Facts are to be acquired via the inquiry process, not as initial instruction with higher-level thinking occurring later if there is time.

A mastery grading scheme could assist in reaching these ambitious goals by specifying clearly which definitions, facts, events, or principles are fundamental to intelligent discourse about the topic of study and how they will be assessed (e.g., by a separate test or by their necessary inclusion in a report). These constitute the *required mastery objectives* to earn a minimum passing grade for the unit. Beyond that, students' inquiry projects, including historical, legal, or cross-cultural research into the topic, can be done as *enrichment activities* to raise grades above minimum. As such, these can be done as individual projects on different topics and with somewhat different goals: as cooperative team projects that raise the grade of each member of the team when satisfactorily completed; as cooperative whole-class efforts culminating, for example, in a United-Nations-style debate of nations' ambassadors, a skit, or some other creative way. An example of a grading rubric for such a unit is provided in Example 2.5.

Assessment of Significant Learning

To be commensurate with multiple instructional goals, assessment must be congruent with the school's stated objectives and be multifaceted. "Knowledge, thinking skills, valuing and social participation" (NCSS, 1994, p. 171) should be assessed in multiple ways, which means "augmenting traditional tests with performance evaluations, portfolios of student papers and projects, and essays focusing on higher order thinking and applications" (NCSS, 1994, p. 172).

The NCSS (1994), like the NCTM and NRC, does endorse any particular teaching or testing method and in its section on assessment mentions that appropriate uses of criterion-referenced and norm-referenced tests should supplement daily monitoring of student progress and quality of participation (pp. 171-172). The NCSS explicitly identifies the primary purpose of such testing as that of improving teaching and learning. Except for its nod to norm-referenced assessment, which, as noted in Chapter 1, has the purpose of comparing students or schools to one another, the NCSS is most concerned about what is taught and learned, along with the processes used and how assessments can provide feedback for improving the teaching and learning. These are paraphrases of mastery learning.

Example 2.5 Rubric for Grading Inquiry in Social Studies Units

The following are two basic grading schemes, one based on letters, the other numerical, designed to motivate students to achieve mastery in understanding basic concepts and conducting and reporting inquiry projects in the social sciences.

Letter Grade	Numerical Grade	Interpretation of Grades
A (A– to A+)	95 (90-100)	Met the standards for B (or 85) *and* demonstrated advanced understanding or application of the concept, including the ability to do research, provide historical or cultural context, and draw appropriate conclusions.
B (B– to B+)	85 (80-89)	Met the standards for C (or 75) *and* generated ideas for applying or teaching the concepts, including logical approaches to the relationship between evidence and explanations.
C (C– to C+)	75 (70-79)	Passed required tests on the fundamental concepts (by scoring at least 80% on paper-and-pencil tests) and can defend at least two points of view on controversial topics.

D (D– to D+)	65 (60-69)	Might be able to pass state minimum competency tests, but (1) demonstrates little understanding of the concepts and applications; and/or (2) is not able to see the logic for more than one point of view or place opinions in cultural context; or does (1) or (2) but not both. Thus has not yet achieved mastery.
F	50	Unlikely to pass state competency tests and thus has not mastered the concepts for this grade level nor adequate inquiry skills.

Using Mastery Learning to Implement the NCSS Standards

There is probably no other field in which knowledge or ideas are so generously endowed with potential relevance or transfer: from one culture to another, from one time period to another, and so on. Concepts such as supply and demand, superior overreach by superpowers, the tyranny of majorities over minorities, individual rights versus the common good, technological change versus traditions, and equity of opportunity, to name a few, seem powerful because they are so widely applicable and so central to analyzing conflicts and exploring potential solutions.

The prefaces to most history textbooks have long emphasized such connectedness and concern for teaching critical thinking, and yet "of more than 61,000 questions found in the teacher guides, student workbooks, and tests for 9 history textbooks, more than 95 percent were devoted to factual recall" (U.S. Department of Education, 1987, p. 48). Let us hope that more current data on text materials would show a more balanced set of activities between acquiring facts and processing them via higher levels of thinking, but hope is no substitute for a plan. Two such plans, using lessons from the NCSS standards, are described below.

A High School Lesson on Cultural Diversity

Consider the example the NCSS presents in its executive summary on culture and cultural diversity, in which students in Bill

Tate's high school class are discussing the issue of prayer in the school.

> One student favors prayer in school, noting that "every important document of this country makes reference to God, and when presidents or judges are sworn in, they place their hands on the Bible." Another student responds that she is a Buddhist, so her concept of God and religion is different from what the first student was talking about. A Muslim student points out that Islam is the fastest growing religion in the world, and asks: "What if Muslims become a religious majority in the U.S.? Which American principle would prevail, majority rule or freedom of religion?" Another chimes in her opinion that freedom of religion really means freedom from state-imposed religion. She points out that the United States is a democracy not a theocracy, and argues that even though God is mentioned in U.S. documents and certain ceremonies, public schools should not sanction any one form of religion.
>
> Tate records students' comments on the board, ensuring that everyone is heard and no one's ideas are ridiculed. As the period ends, he presents a case study about a city's decision to place a nativity scene on public property. For homework and discussion the next day, students are to determine whether they agree or disagree with the decision, list reasons supporting their opinion, and research analogous historical or contemporary situations. (NCSS, 1994, p. xv)

Although this discussion appears quite sensible, even profound, due to the well-articulated positions and diverse views of the students, it is not at all clear whether anything was learned. The students, after all, are only stating their own previously held positions, and no one has had to summarize another's position as required in dialogical thinking or conflict resolution (mentioned previously). In addition, Mr. Tate's follow-up assignments likewise emphasize already held positions rather than (a) walking a mile in another person's beliefs or (b) becoming better informed about the topic in general.

Regarding information, recent data collected by Harris-Ewing (1999) show that preservice teachers are, first, mostly ignorant of the laws concerning teaching religion and prayer in schools; second, know very little about religions other than their own (and many are misinformed about their own); and third, recognize their lack of preparation for this significant aspect of people's lives. If prospective teachers are mostly unprepared, one can hardly expect high school students to have the prerequisites. Wouldn't it, therefore, be facilitative of, if not absolutely necessary for, a discussion of a home-work position statement to learn at least (a) what the Supreme Court and other legal precedents say about religion and prayer in the schools and (b) some fundamental beliefs of four or five of the world's religions? These could easily be required for a mastery test on this unit.

Then, if we want to expand our students' thinking beyond the comprehension level, we would give homework or enrichment assignments such as the following:

- Pick a religion other than your own and pretend that you are the lawyer in front of the Supreme Court defending that religion's position about prayer in the schools. What are the major points that need to be made?

- Summarize your position about prayer in the schools. Then critique it from the point of view of another religion.

- State the fundamental beliefs regarding prayer in the schools by at least two religions and by atheists. Suggest a policy on prayer to which all might agree.

- Provide examples of two religions using different language to express the same or similar beliefs. For example: The Five Pillars of Islam are the minimum sacred obligations on all Muslims if they are to properly follow their faith. The first is the belief in the *Shehada*, the statement in Arabic that says, "There is no god but God (Allah) and Muhammad is His Prophet," with *Allah* being the Arabic word for God. Similarly, Christians are guided by the Ten Commandments, the first of which states, "I am the Lord your God. . . . You shall have no other gods before me."

Although it is possible for students to take responsibility for their own learning in some of these ways while doing Mr. Tate's assign-ment, in practice, it will be the rare student who does so. If all students are to "have access to the full richness of the social studies curriculum" (NCSS, 1994, p. 162) and the teaching and learning is to be "challenging" (p. 167), then we must move beyond discussions and exercises in which people simply practice articulating their preexisting opinions.

Suggestions for a mastery learning grading plan for this unit are given in Example 2.6.

Example 2.6 A Mastery Grading Scheme for the NCSS High School Example on Prayer in the Schools

The following are the steps involved in planning a mastery grading scheme for the lesson described in the text (thinking levels are categorized by Bloom's and Marzano's taxonomies, respectively):

1. Decide what is fundamental to understanding (for which all students will be held accountable) and what is enrichment (which may be optional). Regarding school prayer, likely fundamentals are as follows:
   a. Laws concerning the relation of religion and public education.
   b. Central beliefs of the major religions of the world.

2. For the fundamentals, provide students with objectives or study questions and invent practice exercises congruent with the instructional materials to facilitate (a) acquisition of the basic facts and definitions (knowledge or retrieval), (b) recognition of these concepts in real world practices (comprehension), and (c) discovery of ways those concepts were historically or currently relevant (application or utilization). Note that this list implies no necessary order: It may be preferable to include the discovery of the need for more knowledge through publicized incidents or legal cases. For example, students could consider the 1963 case of *Abington v. Schempp,* in which the Supreme Court ruled that religious exercises must pass the test that their primary purpose and impact must be secular rather than religious (Harris-Ewing, 1999, p. 13).
   a. Devise mastery tests on these fundamentals, which (like the driver's test) must be passed at a standard of 75% or 80% correct. These can often be objective tests (short answer, matching, or multiple choice) or one- or two-paragraph essays with a scoring key detailed enough to diagnose the students' abilities to apply the concepts to real situations.
   b. Design and schedule activities for students who do not pass the mastery test as well as parallel forms for retesting.

3. For the enrichment objectives, supply a list of projects that students may do to apply these concepts to new cases, analyze or diagnose events based on the concepts, invent alternative conceptions or ways to resolve conflicts, or teach others (including fellow students in 2b) about these concepts and their applicability. These can be done in cooperative teams or individually, presented as reports, and/or included in student portfolios. Four examples of such enrichment projects are described in the text. A fifth might be to have students report on additional legal cases, both federal and in your state.

4. Grade the students on the unit (as described in the "Discussion and Conclusions" section of Chapter 1). For example, a grade of C or 70 would be earned for passing the mastery test on the unit, with additional points or a higher grade being awarded for each additional project (5 or 10 points; a B for tutoring another student, awarded when the tutee passes; and 10-15 points or an A for an inquiry-based case study analysis).

Elementary and Middle School Lessons on Distribution and Consumption

"Production, Distribution, and Consumption" is the seventh theme of the NCSS standards, and two lessons, one from the early grades and one from the middle grades, provide the content for what follows. In his fourth-grade class, Pete Vlahos demonstrates the complexities of world trade by dividing his class into seven "countries." Each needs building materials for a government building, but they discover that not all of these materials are produced within their country.

> Each country group is given a large bag with supplies, tasks, and discussion sheets. When the groups take out the supplies allocated to them, they find that other groups have more, fewer, or different supplies than they have. One group registers its frustration with having only a bottle of glue and a pair of scissors. This group soon learns, however, that these commodities are in great demand and, through some savvy

trading, the students are able to acquire needed materials, but implementing effective trading strategies is the ultimate measure of success.

Upon completion of the task, the groups reconvene as a class, and students discuss how they felt when they saw the disparities in resources from one country to another, what problems they encountered in trading, how this activity mirrors the real world, and how trading helps or hinders countries. Vlahos evaluates the success of the lesson by asking students to provide other examples of how the U.S. economic system is connected to or dependent upon other countries. (NCSS, 1994, p. 66)

In her sixth-grade class, Patti Barbes wants students to understand the difficulties associated with food distribution, even for crisis situations or especially at-risk populations in the world.

She divides the class into six working groups and gives each group an apple. Each group must decide who will get the apple. There are initial shouts of "Me! Me! Me!" In one group, the first person to grab the apple refuses to give it up. These initial reactions give way to intense discussions about dividing the apples, a coin toss is proposed, and one group tries to determine who has the greatest need.

After each group shares its solutions and its difficulties in coming to a conclusion, Barbes asks each student to consider how the group's deliberations might have been different if they all were experiencing a very limited and inadequate diet. After students write their reactions in their journals, Barbes leads a discussion of their reactions. (NCSS, 1994, p. 97)

The NCSS (1994) performance expectations for this theme include "how scarcity and choice govern our economic decisions" and "the relationship of price to supply and demand," to name two that are relevant to both lessons (p. 41). However, it is far from clear how these "expectations" will be assessed in the lessons described. In other words, despite these interesting and creative activities, we have not assessed whether individual students have learned even the fundamentals of supply and demand, let alone the ability to apply their knowledge to other situations.

Both of these lessons would benefit from a clear articulation of (a) what specifically should be learned from these exercises and (b) what prior knowledge is required. If understanding issues of supply and demand are not prerequisites, then they are surely expected outcomes that can be assessed in mastery tests or as part of inquiry projects (as described in Examples 2.5 and 2.6).

We now turn our attention to our fourth and final set of national learning standards, those for the English language arts.

English Language Arts Standards

Overview

The *Standards for the English Language Arts* were published in 1996,

To define, as clearly and specifically as possible, the current consensus among literacy teachers and researchers about what students should learn in the English language arts— reading, writing, listening, speaking, viewing, and visually representing. The ultimate purpose of these standards is to ensure that *all* students are offered the opportunities, the encouragement, and the vision to develop the language skills they need to pursue life's goals, including personal enrich- ment and participation as informed members of our society. (IRA/NCTE, 1996, p. 1; italics in original)

A joint project of the International Reading Association (IRA) and the National Council of Teachers of English (NCTE) and supported initially by a Department of Education grant, the standards evolved over a 4-year period to provide a "shared vision of literacy educa- tion" (IRA/NCTE, 1996, pp. 6-8). That vision includes the content knowledge and learning strategies students need, along with curric- ular developments and instructional strategies to facilitate students' progress.

The standards are introduced (IRA/NCTE, 1996, p. 3) as a list of 12 propositions, which are later elaborated to emphasize their inter- relatedness and encourage an eclectic mix of methods (pp. 27-46). Several of the 12 standards *emphasize breadth of exposure to literature:* both fiction and nonfiction, classic and contemporary (#1); from genres ranging from the philosophical to the aesthetic (#2); and from spoken, written, and visual media (#4). Several *emphasize the produc- tive uses or purposes of literacy:* to comprehend, interpret, evaluate, or appreciate text (#3); to communicate with different audiences (#4, #5); to generate ideas, conduct research, and communicate findings (#7); to appreciate diversity (#9); to increase capabilities for using technology and other resources (#8); and for the ability to participate fully in society and for personal fulfillment (#11, #12). Others *emphasize the skills that need to be developed:* learning and comprehension strategies (#3); language structure and conventions, vocabulary, spelling, punctuation, styles, and figurative language (#4, #6); writing strategies (#5); technological and research skills (#8); and competency in English as a second language (#10).

The 12 standards are further interpreted through an interactive model (IRA/NCTE, 1996, Chapter 2), in which the learner's development interacts with specific intent, instructional purpose, and the general context (social and cultural). All of these must be considered in developing curricula, activities, assessments, and strategies. As more of these components are realized, we come closer to the idealized classroom imagined for the English language arts:

> Students are engaged in small groups and individual research projects that link classroom and academic inquiry to their lived social and family experiences. They tell each other stories, argue constructively, share resources, read newspaper articles aloud to one another, make collages and videotapes, and write letters and essays. Displays of students' writing and graphics welcome visitors to the classroom and enhance students' sense of being part of a vital language community both within and beyond the school. (IRA/NCTE, 1996, p. 46)

Links to Mastery

As with the NCTM, NRC, and NCSS, equity is offered as both a fundamental principle and raison d'etre for the IRA/NCTE standards. Along with equity, three other pervasive links to mastery learning are assessments that complement rather than drive instruction, rubrics, and metacognitive processes to help students learn to learn. Let's consider each of these four in turn.

1. "To Promote Equity and Excellence for All"

In the section with the above title, the IRA/NCTE (1996) standards proclaim,

> In a democracy, free and universal schooling is meant to prepare *all* students to become literate adults capable of critical

thinking, listening and reading, and skilled in speaking and writing. (p. 8)

They go on to describe how easy it is to fail the powerless, the economically disadvantaged, and medically or psychologically at-risk populations. These disadvantages can become opportunities, the standards go on to say, when we value differences in linguistic patterns and abilities and also recognize and adapt our instruction to allow faster and slower students the time they need to attain the high standards.

These statements are fully consistent with mastery philosophy and John Carroll's model of school learning, described previously, in which all students can learn the basics of most courses and student aptitude is a measure of rate of attaining course objectives, rather than amount or level of complexity attainable.

2. "Performance-Based Assessment" versus "Preparing for Machine-Scored Tests"

The standards only indirectly address assessment issues (refer-ring the reader instead to a separate document, IRA/NCTE, 1994) in the following manner:

> While many teachers wish to gauge their students' learning using performance-based assessment, they find that prepar-ing students for machine-scored tests which often focus on isolated skills rather than contextualized learning diverts valuable classroom time away from the development of actual performance. (IRA/NCTE, 1996, p. 7)

This presumes that important skills such as recognizing words and comprehending passages at the elementary level and use of cor-rect punctuation and language conventions at more advanced levels can all be assessed in contextualized projects in which the literacy performance is creative writing, critical analysis, or drama.

But reliability, validity, and efficiency of scoring, which imply accuracy of diagnosis, feedback, and improvement of students, require that mechanics and content be assessed independently. When they are all combined, scores on the same essay are uninter-pretable: For example, an 80 could be obtained by a poor writer who knows the content well or by a test-wise student whose good writ-ing ability masks weak comprehension of the topic. In a demonstra-tion of these problems, teachers who developed rubrics and scored essays, not knowing they were all scoring the very same essay, found their evaluations covered the entire range from excellent to dismal failure, from almost no points to maximum points (Gentile, 2000a).

Separating performance skills from content knowledge has a long history in many fields: The driver's test has a performance test as well as a multiple-choice test on rules of the road; Olympic skaters are judged separately on skills and aesthetic presentations; and teachers must not only write acceptable lesson plans but must also teach those lessons. The virtue of requiring that each of these domains be assessed separately, in addition to providing more efficacious scoring, is that it provides better feedback on which aspects of a complex task need improvement.

Writing an essay is certainly exemplary among complex tasks. In fact, some would argue it is synonymous with thinking. That is the reason measurement texts (e.g., Airasian, 1994; Gronlund, 1993) recommend that essays not be wasted on assessing knowledge or comprehension levels of Bloom's (1956) taxonomy (retrieval or comprehension in Marzano, 2001). These can efficiently be tested by objective tests as such two-choice, multiple-choice, matching, and short-answer items. Rather, essays should be reserved for testing the application, analysis, synthesis, and evaluation levels of thinking, perhaps also including appreciation (analysis, utilization, and self levels in Marzano's taxonomy). An essay, which by this logic assesses higher levels of thinking about some literature or concept, must therefore be assessed differently from a performance test of the art of writing in which style and creativity take precedence over content knowledge.

Consistent with the mastery learning perspective of this book, in which mastery of critical basic skills is the initial learning that enables further development via more individualized enrichment activities, it is necessary to identify those basic skills and knowledges and require that minimum standards on them be met. This can be accomplished in more than one way, however, as illustrated below:

- Have regularly scheduled mastery tests on spelling, grammar, punctuation, vocabulary, language conventions, and other features of form or style (e.g., business letters). These must be passed separately from the essays, which require higher-level thinking, or writing performances, such as letters or poems, which involve creativity or aesthetics.

- Assess students only on their "authentic" literary projects, be they dramatic productions, poetry, essays, or reports, but then require that these be edited to be perfect regarding spelling, grammar, punctuation, and style. Only then do students get credit for the project and/or can the item be included in a student's portfolio or displayed in school.

3. Rubrics

It follows from the previous section that evaluating writing performances or inquiry projects in the language arts is no easy task. Thus it is necessary to develop some form of rubric, defined as the criteria for judging or scoring a complex performance, including examples (or anchors) of what constitutes competence at each scoring level for each component of the performance (e.g., Arter & McTighe, 2001). Although one could probably invent ways of using rubrics in a norm-referenced fashion, the fundamental purposes of using rubrics is to help teachers (and students) answer the following questions for criterion-referenced purposes:

- What is expected?
- What are our standards?
- What does good performance look like?
- What do I want to accomplish?
- What kind of feedback do I give to improve student work next time?
- Where are my students in their journey to competence, and what is the next step in instruction?
- Is my instruction effective? (Arter & McTighe, 2001, p. 11)

Useful rubrics for the language arts are described in Arter and McTighe (2001), IRA/NCTE (1994), and the New York State Standards (NYSED, 1996), in which they are described as "performance indicators." Criteria for rubrics are provided in Example 2.7.

4. Teaching for "Learning How to Learn"

In a section on "Learning How to Learn" in NCTE's Chapter 1, the standards adopt the following position:

All students have the ability to learn, but teachers can make that ability accessible by helping students reflect upon, and monitor, their own learning. When students see themselves as able learners, capable of monitoring and controlling their learning, they are more willing to tackle challenging tasks and

Example 2.7   Criteria for English Language Arts Rubrics for Mastery Learning Purposes

A rubric needs to adequately cover the content to be judged; to ignore nonessential content; to be sufficiently clear and comprehensible so as to be interpreted in the same way by students and teachers; and to be practical, defined as not too complicated to be used (Arter & McTighe, 2001). In the English language arts, different rubrics are likely to be needed for each of the many domains of the field, for example, reading, writing, speaking, and drama, and each has to be congruent with specific curriculum goals if it is to be criterion referenced.

The following are illustrative of the kinds of criteria and dimensions that might be considered for a rubric for an inquiry project culminating in a written report. This particular rubric is based on New York State's "performance indicators" for a ninth-grade assignment to research a topic and then write a story about it (NYSED, 1996a, p. 46). In the example given, a student invented a story of the "My Lai Massacre" as a child might have experienced it.

Level of Performance

	*Advanced (2 points)**	*Mastery (1 point)**	*Nonmastery (0 points)**
Dimensions	Satisfies all criteria Needs no revisions or only cosmetic changes to be complete.	Meets minimum passing standards or initial mastery; may need significant changes for portfolio or display.	Has not yet reached minimum standards; needs additional work in areas noted.
Quality of research	Evident analysis of texts for details, well organized into a	Shows evidence of comprehension and use of texts to derive background material,	Little evidence of use of research in the story developed, either by

	context for the student's story. Well beyond initial mastery level.	which is reasonably integrated into the story.	lack of comprehension of text or little ability to organize or synthesize the facts.
Quality of story	Coherent story that portrays the historical texts in a creative or humanly compelling way. Well beyond initial mastery level.	Writing is both appropriate to the research and tells a story in narrative form with imagery and good character development.	Story has little or no form, imagery, or character development or is not internally consistent.
English usage	Uses standard English, a broad and precise vocabulary, idioms, metaphors, etc. Well beyond initial mastery level.	Uses standard English with adequate grasp of vocabulary and idioms; uses full sentences and coherent paragraphs; spelling; conventions of language are correct or appropriate to the story.	Uses nonstandard English, very limited or poor choice of vocabulary; sentences are incomplete or run-on; little understanding of idioms.
Writing mechanics	Grammar, spelling, punctuation, and conventions	At least 80% of grammar, vocabulary, spelling, and conventions	Too many errors (more than 20%) in grammar,

of language are all correct or appropriate to the story.	of language are correct or appropriate to the story.	vocabulary, spelling, and conventions of language.

*Please note that the points suggested above can be summed to yield a range of 0-8 (e.g., advanced scores in each of the four categories: $2 \times 4 = 8$; Nonmastery: $0 \times 4 = 0$), as is traditional for such rubrics. But in keeping with the mastery grading arguments of this book, each domain must be corrected to at least mastery before summing the scores. A 2 each in research and story telling do not compensate for 0 in each of the other categories. When English usage and mechanics are each revised to earn scores of 1, then a summed grade of 6 $(2 + 2 + 1 + 1)$ is logical and consistent with the mastery goals, whereas $2 + 2 + 0 + 0 = 4$ is not.

Alternatively, mastery-level performance in each category could receive the lowest passing grade (as in Examples 2.2 and 2.4), and advanced work could raise the unit grade as an enrichment paper.

Please note also that we could have used standard labels such as "excellent" or "honors" for what we called "advanced." Whatever label it is given, it must not be interpreted in norm-referenced fashion (i.e., instead of "above average," it must be criterion referenced as in "beyond initial mastery toward true expertise").

take the risks that move their learning forward. (IRA/NCTE, 1996, p. 9)

This position is supported later in a section entitled "Development," in which language learning is described as an active developmental process to make sense of the world, as a very individualized process that builds on prior experience and goes at different rates, and as a socially mediated process.

The first step in literacy education, then . . . is to respect each student's home language, prior knowledge, and cultural experience, and to determine what he or she already knows and can do upon entering school. Teachers must then provide appropriate and rich instructional support on that basis. (IRA/NCTE, 1996, p. 20)

These two quotations and the prose surrounding them are firmly grounded in theory, some of which was already described in Chapter 1 (notably, learned helplessness theory and its antidote, learned competence; Carroll's definition of aptitude; and the importance of prerequisites for mastery). In addition, the standards make metacognitive processes central to learning to learn, which also has empirical and theoretical support for emerging literacy in work such as Palinscar and Brown's (1984) reciprocal teaching for comprehension monitoring, Vygotsky's (1962) theory of the development of thought through language, and Marzano's (2001) taxonomy.

Consider Vygotsky's defense of instruction in grammar and phonetics against critics of such instruction. He argued that when a Russian student learns that the word *Moscow* is comprised of separate sounds or that sentences are constructions of recognizable component parts, that person "becomes aware of what he is doing and learns to use his skills consciously" (Vygotsky, 1962, p. 101). This argument is notable on two accounts: First, it was an early statement on the importance of *metacognition* (before Flavell, 1979, popularized the word) as active, conscious self-monitoring of what the student knows and does not know, remembers and does not recall, and so forth. Second, it was an argument supportive of the necessity of mastering basic component skills for higher-level literacy goals. The "appropriate and rich instructional support" cited above, which Vygotsky would call "learning in a zone of proximal development," is necessarily individualized to go at the student's best pace with tasks that are just beyond what the student can now do.

Using Mastery to Implement IRA/NCTE Standards

The IRA/NCTE standards provide neither exemplary lessons nor specific ways to assess the outcomes of those lessons. Instead, they present (in Chapter 4) several vignettes for elementary, middle, and secondary classrooms to provide for "further reflections on the standards" and to "highlight both the complexities and the serendipities of literacy learning" (IRA/NCTE, 1996, p. 47). Following each vignette are two or three questions designed to provide additional opportunities for teacher reflection. Let's consider two of these vignettes.

Teaching Reading Strategies

In "Elementary Vignette 7," Mrs. D. is teaching her upper elementary students

> A mini-lesson on reading strategies. She tells the students that she often stops her reading at particular points in a story to picture scenes or characters in her head. She explains that this helps her understand the characters and gives her a better sense of the place and the time of the story. At the end of the lesson, Mrs. D. invites her students to try this strategy as they read a book of their own choosing. After spending a few minutes circulating . . . the students and teacher read independently.
>
> Eight minutes before the end of the class period, the students gather for a sharing time. The teacher begins, as she always does, by asking, "How did it go today?" (IRA/NCTE, 1996, p. 54)

Mrs. D.'s question induces a few volunteers to describe their experiences, which stimulates comments about the visualization strategy as well as other strategies. Finally, the teacher summarizes: "One strategy does not work in every situation. . . . Readers need to make flexible use of a range of strategies" (p. 54). The vignette concludes with two questions for further reflection:

- How does discussion about reading strategies help students gain greater competence and independence as readers?
- What should a teacher do for students who overrely on one strategy? (IRA/NCTE, 1996, p. 54)

These are both good questions for which mastery learning has suggestions. First note, however, that in the lesson described in the standards, Mrs. D. discovered only how the volunteers reported using the visualization strategy. Although she *described* her own use of the strategy, she did not *model* it; then she provided no practice using the strategy before or during the independent reading and certainly did no assessment to be able to answer for her students the two reflection questions on which the IRA/NCTE wish her to reflect.

Please note that the above is not a critique of independent reading; it is just to say that by definition, independent reading cannot answer the questions posed. Rather, Mrs. D.'s independent reading needs to be supplemented by mini-lessons that more directly practice and assess, at various levels of thinking, the strategies to be acquired.

Consider the following illustrative lessons (labeled for level of thinking in the Bloom and Marzano taxonomies, respectively):

1. Think-Pair-Share Strategy Lesson: Have students first list strategies and describe how they work, then compare their list with those of one or two partners (*knowledge/retrieval*). To complete this think-pair-share exercise, these ideas can then be discussed with the whole class. To monitor what individuals have learned, the teacher can (a) collect the students' initial lists, (b) have students expand their lists after the discussions and then collect them, (c) give a short quiz on these strategies, and (d) require that students continue to revise their page of strategies for inclusion in their portfolios, and so forth.

2. Guided Practice on a Strategy: Give students an appropriate page or two to read while using a new reading strategy, such as Mrs. D.'s visualization strategy. Then have them each write a few lines on (a) what they learned from the pages and (b) how well the strategy worked to help them learn it (*comprehension* and *application/ utilization*; plus practice with *metacognition*). Excerpts from these notes can be shared with small groups or the whole class. Then they can be rewritten for their portfolios.

3. Additional Strategies: The techniques in #2 can be repeated for various strategies with the additional requirement that students compare one strategy with another in terms of (a) fundamental similarities and differences, (b) their efficacy for comprehending text, and/or (c) the students' personal preferences regarding them (*evaluation/analysis* and *self*).

4. Case Study Diagnosis: Provide students with a case study of a hypothetical student who is having difficulty comprehending text. Have students diagnose what is likely to be wrong, such as lack of an appropriate reading strategy or misused strategy. Then, perhaps after first discussing what is wrong, assign students to create a plan for remediating the student's problem (*analysis* and *synthesis/analysis*). For examples of case studies, see Example 2.8.

5. Metacognition Lesson: Teach students the differences between cognitive and metacognitive strategies: For example, if visualization is a cognitive strategy for comprehending, then asking oneself "How well I comprehended," "Whether I used the strategy well or not," and "How well it worked," are metacognitive strategies. Then provide practice exercises (*application* and *analysis/ metacognition*).

Example 2.8   A Case Study for Teaching Strategies of Reading

---

Following are two hypothetical cases for students to diagnose to help them learn about, apply, and analyze reading strategies (as described in "Teaching Reading Strategies"):

1. Craig seems very interested in the reading and writing assignments in English, and he is constantly checking himself on whether he knows how to spell the new words in the text or gets punctuation right in his writing. However, he rarely passes even the easiest test about the content of the text. What is Craig's problem? How can he be helped to correct it?

2. Whenever Jeanetta takes a reading test, she reads the passage once and then tries to answer all the questions, even if she can't remember or didn't learn the material in the passage. When her teacher asked her what else she could do, she shrugged her shoulders. What is Jeanetta's problem? How can she be helped to correct it?

Inquiry Via Literature

In "High School Vignette 2," students are reading Chinua Achebe's *Things Fall Apart* and Alan Paton's *Cry, The Beloved Country*, set in colonial Nigeria and South Africa, respectively.

> For most of the students, these two books have been their first experience with African literature . . . and they have become deeply interested in the history of Africa, its colonization by European nations, and the politics of racial apartheid in South Africa. . . .
>
> Drawing on the personal impact of racist policies on characters in the two novels, students have opened up many conversations about the experience of racial identity and difference as it has shaped their own lives. To address the many questions they have raised, *several* students in the class have decided to put together a multimedia presentation for their classmates. (IRA/NCTE, 1996, pp. 61-62; italics added)

This class has rich resources available, including a video camera, computer technology, and reference material for easy search of history, geography, and even music of the regions. Thus they include music, a dance by one of the participants, and a voice-over script written by two students, and they present the piece 2 weeks later to their class.

Of the three questions for teacher reflection at the end of the vignette, two are relevant to this discussion. The first concerns how technology can empower students to produce such works, as well as how such a project would be adapted to classes with fewer or no technological advantages. The second asks how to deal with students' personal experiences and concerns over difficult issues such as racism in an open and honest way.

From our mastery learning vantage point, here are several suggestions that improve this worthwhile inquiry project. First, consider how to include all students instead of just the two scriptwriters and several other members of a project team. Apparently all students read the novels, so why not make each do some writing as a piece for their portfolios, even if they are not also included in the final production? For example, each student could invent a hypothetical talk show debate between two characters in the novels, a British bureaucrat and a Nigerian debating one of the colonial policies. This use of the dialogical thinking technique (see the NCSS standards, "A High School Lesson on Cultural Diversity") would inform each student of the logic used by opposing sides and possibly suggest ideas for the final production. In addition to giving each student more writing practice, it takes advantage of the idea that writing invites thinking—perhaps eliciting the best thinking humans ever do—in this case at the analysis, synthesis, and metacognitive levels of thinking.

As a second suggestion, consider the benefits of students doing a reflective piece about their project as a drama critic or coach might do. Who was its intended audience? Did it succeed in communicating with that audience? Were all the media, music, dance, narration, scenery, and technical support congruent? What were the strong and weak points of the project? Such a reflection exercise would be an excellent enrichment project in the kinds of grading schemes proposed earlier.

Finally, note that exercises designed to dramatize human communication or conflict involve purposeful uses of speaking or writing errors, inappropriate colloquialisms or expletives, emotion masquerading as logic, and so forth. These provoke students to reflect on the appropriate and/or culturally and socially sensitive uses of language and make conscious decisions about when and why erroneous

---

Example 2.9   Language Arts Portfolios as Demonstrations of
Mastery

Portfolios have long been the quintessential criterion-referenced assessment tool, especially for artists, musicians, architects, and the professoriate, to name a few. As collections of a person's best work or performances, they display competencies, as well as changes or periods in that person's professional life. In a language arts class, portfolios serve those same purposes but should probably also add a reflection component: to have students organize or categorize pieces, to provide a rationale for each piece, and to comment on their own growth as writers.

Based on the above logic, the following might be useful components of a language arts portfolio:

1. The student's own favorite piece of writing, along with a reflection on why it was selected.
2. A reflective piece (creative or informative) stimulated by a favorite book or dramatic work.
3. A collection of reflections, with examples, on language structure or conventions: for example, the newly learned or rediscovered importance of metaphor in good writing; the historical roots of a word and its many uses; or the applications of a rule of grammar or punctuation.
4. A set of revisions or drafts to show the evolution of thinking and writing as a process.
5. Descriptions of reading strategies (as described in "Teaching Reading Strategies").
6. A dialogical thinking piece, to demonstrate both content knowledge about a topic being studied as well as writing skill (as described in "Inquiry via Literature").
7. A creative piece in any genre or medium.

Regarding grading, if each piece were graded with feedback when it was produced, then it can simply be improved, corrected for writing mechanics or content, and included in the portfolio without an additional grade. Alternatively, the portfolio itself could be an enrichment project that raises the students' grade one level when it is satisfactorily completed (e.g., Gentile, 1997).

Otherwise, the portfolio evaluation is like evaluating any piece of writing or work of art: It needs a rubric (such as in Example 2.7).

conventions are best abandoned. This is practice with metacognitive processes, as in the Vygotsky example above, and would make another excellent addition to a portfolio (see Example 2.9 for other ideas).

Summary

In this chapter, learning standards developed by national organizations in the areas of math, science, social studies, and English language arts were presented and critiqued with respect to their relations to mastery learning. It was clear in each case that each set of standards was well conceived and well intentioned. Indeed, each recognized the importance of all students learning and of learning being extended beyond the level of rote memorization, consistent with the Bloom and Marzano taxonomies (presented at the beginning of the chapter). Similarly, each provided vignettes and examples of stimulating classroom activities intended to demonstrate ways of implementing their respective standards. Unfortunately, these stimulating learning activities fell short of the intent of their respective standards in several ways. For example, there were no activities to assess students' prior knowledge of essential concepts; there was no assessment of whether students actually learned what they were supposed to learn; and what passed for inquiry or high-level thinking was more akin to expressing their own preexisting opinions. These lessons can be even more effectively aligned with learning standards by including elements of mastery learning to ensure that students are successful at meeting those standards. In modifying some of the national organizations' lessons in this chapter to include elements of mastery, it was our goal to make already good instructional activities into comprehensive and effective lessons. In the next chapter, we will further examine such elements as they relate to detailed lessons in various content areas.

Notes

1. Ways to represent the fraction three-eighths:
   a. As a portion of a whole ■ ■ ■ ☐ ☐ ☐ ☐ ☐
   b. As a quotient: 3/8 or 8$\overline{\smash{\big)}\,3}$

c. As a point on a number line:

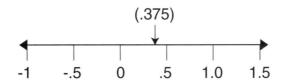

d. In some other way:
   As a ratio: 3 is to 8 as 6 is to 16
   As a percentage: 37.5%
   As a musical notation:

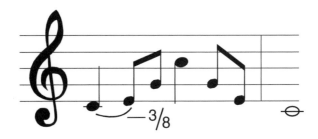

2. Ways to demonstrate that 4/5 divided by 3/8 equals 2.13:

   a. $4/5 \div 3/8 = \dfrac{4/5 \times 8/3}{3/8 \times 8/3} = \dfrac{4/5 \times 8/3}{1} = 4/5 \times 8/3 = \dfrac{32}{15} = 2.13$

   b. Analogous to 5 divided by 2: how many 2's go into 5? How many 3/8ths go in 4/5?

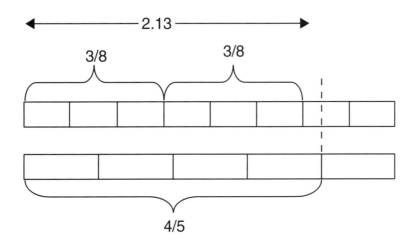

3

Planning Standards-Based Lessons Using Mastery Learning

In this chapter, it is our goal to demonstrate that mastery learning applies to virtually all learning standards. We begin by providing an examination of state and national standards and the overlap among them. We then turn our attention to two key components of any mastery learning system: enrichment and remediation. Finally, we provide some examples that connect the standards with essential activities of mastery learning.

Overlap Among State and National Standards

To this point, our discussion has focused on the national learning standards developed by agencies such as the National Council for the Teaching of Mathematics (NCTM) and the National Council for the Social Studies (NCSS). We have chosen to address the national standards in an attempt to make our discussion applicable to a national, and even international, audience. Although the majority of primary and secondary educators in U.S. schools need to concern themselves with their states' learning standards, we were concerned that a discussion focusing on the learning standards of one or two states would appear applicable to educators from only those states. To allay any concerns that the information regarding learning standards and mastery learning may not apply to a given set of state standards, in this section, we will draw parallels among various state and national standards in an effort to demonstrate that mastery learning will work equally well with either. One should also note that it is likely that those charged with developing standards at the state and local levels relied on national standards to guide them during that process. For example, the standards developed by the NCSS (1994) were designed explicitly for that purpose: "The social studies standards will help teachers, program and curriculum designers, and administrators at the state, district and school-site levels develop a systematic K-12 social studies program" (p. 16). For another example, a portion of the New York State Standards for Social Studies (1996c) was explicitly adapted from the National History Standards (1996), which were developed by another national organization, the National Center for History in the Schools; and the mathematics component of the Illinois Learning Standards (Illinois State Board of Education, 1997) was developed using the NCTM standards. To further corroborate the notion of considerable overlap among state and national standards, consider California's description of their process of developing *the Science Content Standards for California Public Schools:*

> The California State Board of Education and the Academic Standards Commission reviewed the *National Science Education Standards, the Benchmarks for Science Literacy,*[1] and science standards and frameworks from numerous local school districts in California, from around the country, and from other nations with successful science education programs. (California State Board of Education, 1998b, p. 8)

Virtually every set of standards, regardless of level or academic discipline, addresses the issue of equity. For example, the National Council of Teachers of English (IRA/NCTE, 1996) states the following: "The vision guiding these standards is that all students must have the opportunities and resources to develop the language skills they need to pursue life's goals and to participate fully as informed, productive members of society" (p. 1). Table 3.1 provides excerpts regarding equity from various state and national standards, and Table 3.2 provides excerpts regarding content from those same standards. The state standards listed were chosen so that major portions

(text continues on page 92)

Table 3.1 Equity as Described by National and State Standards

NCSS[1]	NCTM[2]	NSES[3]	Florida[4]	New York[5]	Kansas[6]	California[7]
The social studies standards should serve as a guide for curriculum decisions by providing performance expectations regarding knowledge, processes, and attitudes essential for all students.	All students deserve an opportunity to understand the power and beauty of mathematics. All students must have access to the highest-quality mathematics instructional programs.	The goals for school science are to educate students who are able to experience the richness and excitement of knowing about and understanding the natural world. Science understanding and ability also will enhance the capability of all students to hold	The schools, districts, colleges of education, postsecondary institutions, and state work collaboratively to provide professional teachers and staff who possess the competencies and demonstrate the performance needed to	All students will meet high standards for academic performance and personal behavior and demonstrate the knowledge and skills required by a dynamic world.	The Kansas State Board of Education promotes student academic achievement by providing educational vision, leadership, opportunity, accountability, and advocacy for all.	We believe all students can learn. All students deserve an equitable opportunity to succeed. All students require a safe, healthy, environment for learning. All students need physical, emotional, and intellectual

(Continued)

Table 3.1 (Continued)

NCSS[1]	NCTM[2]	NSES[3]	Florida[4]	New York[5]	Kansas[6]	California[7]
		meaningful and productive jobs in the future.	maximize learning among all students.			support from their schools, families, and communities to succeed.

1. National Council for the Social Studies (NCSS, 1994).
2. National Council of Teachers of Mathematics (NCTM, 2000).
3. National Research Council (NRC, 1996).
4. Florida Department of Education (1999).
5. New York State Education Department (2002).
6. Kansas State Board of Education (2001).
7. California Department of Education (2002).

Table 3.2 National and State Content Standards

	National[1]	Florida[2]	New York[3]	Kansas[4]	California[5]
Social Studies: Cultural Diversity	Social studies programs should include experiences that provide for the study of culture and cultural diversity. In a democratic and multicultural society, students need to understand multiple perspectives that derive from different cultural vantage points. This understanding will allow them to relate to people in our nation and throughout the world.	The student understands the history of Florida and its people; understands the reasons that immigrants came to Florida and the contributions of immigrants to the state's history; understands the perspectives of diverse cultural, ethnic, and economic groups with regard to past and current events in Florida's history.	Students: Compare and contrast the experiences of different groups in the United States; examine how the Constitution, United States law, and the rights of citizenship provide a major unifying factor in bringing together Americans from diverse roots and traditions	The student understands the shared ideals and the diversity of American society and political culture; understands that civic values are influenced by people's beliefs and needs (e.g., need for safety, health, and well-being); describes the similarities and unique qualities of cultures in the United States.	Students recognize the ways in which they are all part of the same community, sharing principles, goals, and traditions despite their varied ancestry; the forms of diversity in their school and community; and the benefits and challenges of a diverse population; compare the beliefs, customs, ceremonies, traditions, and social practices of the varied cultures.

(Continued)

Table 3.2 (Continued)

	National[6]	Florida[7]	New York[8]	Kansas[9]	California[10]
Science: Inquiry	Students can investigate earth materials, organisms, and properties of common objects; use their observations to construct reasonable explanations for the questions posed; in elementary grades, students begin to develop the physical and intellectual abilities of scientific inquiry.	Student uses the scientific processes and habits of mind to solve problems; knows that scientific knowledge is subject to modification; new information challenges prevailing theories and new theory leads to looking at old observations in a new way; the study of the events that led scientists to discoveries can provide information about the inquiry process and its effects.	Students attempt to seek greater understanding concerning objects and events they have observed and heard about; develop relationships among observations to construct descriptions of objects and events and to form their own tentative explanations of what they have observed.	Students describe objects and events, ask questions, construct explanations, test those explanations against current scientific knowledge; identify assumptions, use critical and logical thinking; consider alternative explanations; actively develop understanding of science, combining scientific knowledge with reasoning and thinking skills.	Scientific progress is made by asking meaningful questions and conducting careful investigations; students should develop their own questions and perform investigations; make predictions based on observed patterns and not random guessing; compare and sort common objects; write or draw descriptions of a sequence of steps, events and observations.

(Continued)

Table 3.2 (Continued)

	National[11]	Florida[12]	New York[13]	Kansas[14]	California[15]
Math: Reasoning and Problem Solving	Students make sense of the world by reasoning and problem solving, and teachers must recognize that young students can think in sophisticated ways. Students are active, resourceful individuals who construct, modify, and integrate ideas by interacting with the physical world and with peers and adults; make connections that clarify and extend their knowledge, adding new meaning to past experiences.	The student understands the effects of operations on numbers and the relationships among these operations, selects appropriate operations, and computes for problem solving; selects appropriate operation to solve specific problems; adds, subtracts, and multiplies whole numbers, decimals, and fractions, including mixed numbers, and divides whole numbers to solve real-world problems.	Deductive and inductive reasoning are used to reach mathematical conclusions. Students use simple logical reasoning to develop conclusions, recognizing that patterns and relationships present in the environment assist them in reaching these conclusions.	Mathematical application indicators are statements that describe how the mathematical knowledge base should be used or applied to a real-world situation. Students make inferences by using deductive, inductive, proportional, or spatial reasoning such as generalizing a pattern, formulating examples, or counterexamples.	Students practice skills, solve problems, apply mathematics to the real world, develop a capacity for abstract thinking, ask and answer questions involving numbers or equations; become mathematical problem solvers who can recognize and solve routine problems readily and can find ways to reach a solution or goal where no routine path is apparent.

(Continued)

Table 3.2 (Continued)

	National[16]	Florida[17]	New York[18]	Kansas[19]	California[20]
English Language Arts: Reading Comprehension	Students apply a wide range of strategies to comprehend, interpret, evaluate, and appreciate texts. They draw on their prior experience, their interactions with other readers and writers, their knowledge of word meaning and of other texts, their word identification strategies, and their understanding of textual features (e.g., sound-letter	The student selects from a variety of simple strategies, including the use of phonics, word structure, context clues, self-questioning, confirming simple predictions, retelling, and using visual clues, to identify words and construct meaning from various texts, illustrations, graphics, and charts.	Students make appropriate and effective use of strategies to construct meaning from print, such as prior knowledge about a subject, structural and context clues, and an understanding of letter-sound relationships to decode difficult words, support inferences about information and ideas with reference to text features, such as	Student uses what he/she already knows about the topic and the type of text to understand what is read; connect predictions with information read; reread as necessary for understanding; compare and contrast information in texts; recognize problem and solution; identify text organizers such	Students identify the basic facts and ideas in what they have read, heard, or viewed; use comprehension strategies (e.g., comparing new information to what is already known). Use pictures and context to make predictions about story content; connect to life experiences the information and events in texts; ask and answer

(Continued)

Table 3.2 (Continued)

National[16]	Florida[17]	New York[18]	Kansas[19]	California[20]
correspondence, sentence structure, context, graphics).		vocabulary and organizational patterns.	as headings, topic, and summary sentences, and graphic features.	questions about essential elements of a text.

1. NCSS (1994).
2. Florida Department of Education (1996d).
3. New York State Education Department (1996c).
4. Kansas State Board of Education (1999a).
5. California State Board of Education (1998a).
6. NRC (1996).
7. Florida Department of Education (1996c).
8. New York State Education Department (1996b).
9. Kansas State Board of Education (2000b).
10. California State Board of Education (1998b).
11. NCTM (2000).
12. Florida Department of Education (1996b).
13. New York State Education Department (1996b).
14. Kansas State Board of Education (1999b).
15. California State Board of Education (1997b).
16. NCTE (1996).
17. Florida Department of Education (1996a).
18. New York State Education Department (1996a).
19. Kansas State Board of Education (2000a).
20. California State Board of Education (1997a).

of the United States were represented. Thus New York represents the Northeast, Kansas the Midwest, California the West, and Florida the South. In Table 3.2, the national standard was taken from the major organization providing standards for that content area. For example, in "Math," "Problem Solving" is taken from the NCTM standards; and in "Science," "Inquiry" is taken from the NRC standards.

As can be seen from the compilation of various national and state level standards, there is considerable overlap among the standards regarding equity and within content domains. Thus we feel confident that the comments made regarding the application of mastery learning to the national professional organizations' standards or a particular state's standards also apply to well-conceived standards at any level of government, and for that matter, any level of education with well-articulated learning goals.

Enrichment and Remediation

Perhaps the best way to begin a discussion about the critical components of enrichment and remediation in a mastery system is to briefly outline the mastery process. As with any instructional system, mastery should begin with solid learning activities developed by a teacher with sufficient content and pedagogical knowledge of the topic. The initial activity should be one that allows the teacher to assess students' prior knowledge of the topic with the concurrent goal of stimulating student interest. Next comes the delivery of instruction, whether instruction is in the form of, for example, demonstration, cooperative learning, or discovery learning. During instruction, formative assessment should be done in the form of questioning students, listening to student conversations, and so on. At the conclusion of the unit's instructional activities, a more formal assessment should be done to determine what has been learned by each individual student (i.e., has each student mastered the critical instructional objectives to a predetermined acceptable level?). This is the point at which mastery systems diverge from more traditional systems. Teachers using a traditional instructional system would provide what would typically be various grades indicative of varied student achievement, with some students failing to achieve instructional objectives that are likely to be critical to future learnings, and move on to the next topic. In a mastery system, however, variations in student achievement are addressed by follow-up activities.

First, let us consider *remediation,* which is required by students who have not met the minimum standard for the critical instructional objectives. The clearest demarcation between these students, regardless of their levels of achievement, and those who have mastered the lesson's objectives is that students in need of remediation will require more instructional time. They will also require a minimum of one additional assessment following remediation. Remediation can be provided in various forms and may include the following:

- Additional examples and/or explanations
- Different teaching methods, such as peer tutoring or, ironically, the opportunity to teach in order to learn
- Review of previously taught materials
- Different media, such as instructional software as opposed to printed texts

Those students who master the critical instructional objectives will also be given additional instructional time and activities. These activities should be designed to allow students to revisit the objectives and allow for necessary overlearning (see "Mastery as a Beginning" in Chapter 2) and not simply as "busy work" given with the intention of keeping these students occupied while the remainder of the class continues to work toward mastery. Therefore, *enrichment* activities can also be done by those who have not yet passed the mastery test. Enrichment can be provided in various forms and may include the following:

1. Independent research on a topic from the lesson, such as researching the two or three most destructive hurricanes following a lesson on such storms

2. Reporting the results of their research to those students who have also mastered the objectives

3. Writing a story that is relevant to the lesson, such as a narrative about a child who experienced and survived a hurricane following a lesson on such storms

4. Peer tutoring

Peer Tutoring

For those who have heard from parents, "I didn't send my child to this school to be taught by other students," we need to offer a different perspective. The purpose of peer tutoring may seem obvious to them: A student who has mastered the objectives for a given lesson tutors a student who has not mastered those same objectives, with the primary purpose of the tutee (the student being tutored) mastering the objectives. However, this clearly is *not* the primary purpose of peer tutoring. Rather, the tutee learning from the tutee can best be described as an ancillary benefit. *The true benefit of peer tutoring is the overlearning of the tutor.* A consideration of the process of teaching something for the first time should demonstrate this point quite nicely: As teachers, we are never fully aware of how little we understand about a topic until we are charged with the task of teaching it to someone else. The cognitive reorganization necessary for us to explain a topic (typically with relevant examples) is perhaps one of the best examples of learning and thinking at the highest levels (similar to the writing example provided in the "English Language Arts" section of Chapter 2). Thus rather than being "busy work" for the tutor, it is likely one of the best learning and metacognitive experiences we can offer him or her. The bottom line, then, is that *peer tutoring should only be done as a learning activity when it is in the best interest of the tutor.*

Remediation and Enrichment: Two Sides of the Same Coin

Having provided definitions and examples of remediation and enrichment, we feel it is appropriate to conclude with our belief regarding their complementary relationship. A commonly held belief regarding mastery is that for it to be successful, there must be a highly effective, if not innovative, remediation component. Although we do not underestimate the importance of remediation, it is our assertion that the strength of any mastery program is contingent on its enrichment component. The reasoning behind this assertion is at least twofold. The first issue is that a common criticism of mastery is that it focuses on those students who initially fail to master the objectives at the expense of more capable students who often easily master those same objectives. One can certainly find examples of this. However, we suggest that poor planning, rather than mastery learning, is at fault. Teachers need to develop engaging enrichment assignments that are pertinent to their objectives and not seen as busy work by students. (We acknowledge that this is challenging and may be time consuming; however, time needed to prepare such activities should decrease as experience with mastery increases and a collection of activities to draw on develops.) Contrarily, students in need of remediation will often need to simply revisit and revise previous assignments and not be in need of additional materials. However, what they likely will need is additional instruction from the teacher or classroom aide. These resources will only be available to these students if other students are engaged in appropriate enrichment activities. Thus a comprehensive enrichment program is not only a critical component of a mastery learning system but also an effective classroom management tool. Furthermore, enrichment activities need not be narrowly defined as something that occurs following mastery. When scheduling permits, it is appropriate to allow students who have yet to master the critical objectives to engage in enrichment activities. This seems appropriate for at least two reasons: (a) The enrichment activities may assist the student in achieving the critical objectives, and (b) the enrichment activities may provide motivation for that student's learning. Of course, the student cannot use these activities in lieu of passing the mastery test; credit for them is given on achievement of mastery.

Planning Lessons Using Six Elements of Mastery Learning

The mastery philosophy, as we have presented it, requires that teachers consider the following in planning and conducting lessons:

- That each lesson is located in the context of a unit, sequence, or spiral curriculum so that it reinforces and builds on prior knowledge while simultaneously establishing the bases for subsequent concepts and intellectual strategies.

- That prerequisite knowledges or skills are explicitly identified so that (a) they can be activated by an anticipatory set or an exercise designed to refresh the students' memories or (b) missing information or misinformation can be diagnosed and retaught so that students are ready for the current lesson.

- That lessons be taught using a variety of methods, with similar variety in exercises and assessments, to increase the probability that students meet both basic and higher-level objectives.

- That crucial objectives required for mastery, and thus for passing the unit, be clearly written and distributed to students (and thus available to parents and others as well).

- That a wide variety of assessments be established within a grading system designed to assure that students demonstrate mastery not just for facts and skills but also for comprehension, application, thinking, and metacognitive strategies to the published mastery standard in at least the following ways: (a) If competence is to be defined as two or more independent but complementary talents (e.g., fluency and speed of multiplication facts regarding fractions and ability to apply these ideas), then students must demonstrate competence in more than one way to pass the unit (e.g., by oral recitation or a timed objective test of problems to be solved and by generating their own word problems or by designing an exercise to teach someone else); and (b) advanced or enrichment activities must be developed, along with a grading rubric (see Examples 2.2, 2.4, 2.5, and 2.7), to motivate students to go beyond initial mastery and strive for true excellence.

• That a plan be established for remediating any students who fail to achieve the required standards for mastery, including students who were absent.

Although this appears to be a long list of difficult decisions, many teachers already include many of these ideas in their lesson plans when they explicitly attempt to make their own lessons congruent with one or more national or state standards. What follows are excerpts from a variety of lessons from many fields and levels of schooling to exemplify each of the above six elements of mastery learning that need teacher decisions.

1. Lessons Are Contextualized in a Spiral Curriculum

Teaching Fractions for Transfer. In Example 2.1, Item 2, we raised the problem of how to demonstrate in at least two ways that 4/5 divided by 3/8 equals 2.13. One way, of course (see Chapter 2, Note 2), is to follow the invert-and-multiply algorithm. Another is to use a visual representation in which the problem is restated as "How many 3/8s are there in 4/5?"

The transfer or continuity-of-curriculum problem, however, begins in early elementary grades when teachers begin teaching the meaning of fractions as parts of whole objects: cakes, pies, apples, and so on. This works fine for initial comprehension of fractions and their application to the "real world" and continues logically and experientially to addition and subtraction: "If Juan has 4/5 of a cake and gives Maria 3/8 of it, how much is left for Juan?" The problem comes to the fore in later grades when students are faced with problems of multiplication and division of fractions, in which the answers are counterintuitively smaller and larger answers, respectively. Inventive students may draw on their past educational experience to ask, "If Juan's 4/5 of a cake is divided by Maria's 3/8, how can we end up with 2.1 cakes?"

But now comes the real impediment for most students: Too many teachers answer, "Well, forget about cakes, we don't do multiplication and division of fractions that way." They answer that way, of course, because they themselves do not know how to represent the problems visually. And far too many teachers do not (see Table 5.1 and the accompanying text). The message that they give to many students is that math is beyond understanding, and moreover, when a teacher tells them, "Trust me, you'll need this stuff later," they do not believe it.

The solution, for students as well as teachers and curriculum developers, is for all to know what went before and what is coming later. Each new lesson must build on previous ones while simultaneously setting the stage for later lessons. Therefore all elementary school teachers need to know how to represent multiplication and division of fractions as cakes as well as in other ways. Thus in this example, if a teacher represents a cake using a circle with four of five equal wedges darkened, he or she must then present the same circle divided into eighths (perhaps with a transparent overlay or as in Chapter 2, Note 2b). He or she must explain their relationship, noting that there is no whole number ratio between the two as there would be if it were 2/4 and 2/8. Thus when 4/5 is divided into 3/8 sections, the lines dividing the cake into eighths will not fall on the lines dividing the same cake into fifths. Therefore one 3/8 section will be just less than 2/5, and a second 3/8 section will be just less than 4/5. Therefore there will be two units of 3/8 and a small portion of a third 3/8 unit making up 4/5. This is how a fraction divided by another fraction results in a larger number than the initial number, or in this case, how 4/5 divided by 3/8 equals 2.13.

The Suzuki Method for Mastering Violin. Violinist Namisi Chilungu[2] reflected on her early instruction on the violin as follows:

> During the first several years that I was learning to play the violin, my teacher would place a cheerio on top of my violin bow as I carefully moved it up and down in the air and watched to make sure that I didn't lose my prize to the carpet below. When I had achieved this feat, and my teacher was convinced that I could balance my bow without losing control, I was allowed to eat the cheerio. More importantly, once I showed that I could do this, and a few other basic violin

exercises consistently (hold the violin under my chin with both arms down by my side, stand with my feet in the appropriate position, use the correct "bow hold," etc.), I was allowed to move on to other tasks. Before I knew it, I was wowing my parents with renditions of "Twinkle, Twinkle, Little Star"—several variations, no less. As a student of the Suzuki Method, I experienced an approach to learning music that systematically incorporated many of the basic concepts that are part of mastery learning.

The Suzuki Method consists of learning pieces of music from a certified Suzuki instructor, beginning with the most basic songs and progressing to more challenging pieces. There are approximately 10 books, and it is the teacher's responsibility to teach the necessary techniques that are required to move forward.

Demonstrating mastery to a high level becomes an inherent part of the Suzuki Method. Although students initially learn pieces by listening, they will eventually be required to learn how to read music and memorize most of the music that they have been taught. It is assumed (and it is my personal experience) that once a student is able to play a piece from memory (or at least very well with the music), he or she has learned it well enough to meet the expected requirements. Not only that, but that student can then begin to surpass the level of basic mastery (knowing all of the notes, counting correctly, etc.) and can begin to develop more creative aspects of the music making that may involve paying closer attention to stylistic details. In addition, once students have demonstrated mastery to a certain level (usually Book 5 or Book 6), they are allowed to audition for an advanced group, which meets weekly to learn additional music outside of the standard repertoire (and sometimes even go on tours). This may be considered the equivalent of an enrichment activity.

The criticism that mastery may hold back faster students also does not seem to affect the Suzuki Method. Most likely, that is because students receive individual instruction in which they essentially determine their own pace by practicing the skills until learned to a high level of mastery. In addition, the group lessons allow better players to serve as examples to players who are less strong. In fact, advanced students are often called on to assist with beginner classes or to pair up with younger students to be a practice partner. Not only does this benefit the younger or less experienced players, but it also gives the older or more experienced player a chance to review pieces and skills learned early on in the Suzuki curriculum.

As Ms. Chilungu describes it, the Suzuki Method is certainly mastery based and criterion referenced, with multi-age classes formed on the basis of similar level of skill and mastery of prerequisite techniques. We have included it as illustrative of the first element of mastery because of her last comment: Suzuki students and teachers continually see where they have been and where they are going in this curriculum. Advanced students help beginning students, thus overlearning their technical skills and understanding the music concepts at a higher level. In addition, they learn harmonies and variations so that they can play along with the beginners. Novices, on the other hand, have role models at all ages, learn to see the benefits of practice, and can aspire to what comes later in the curriculum. At any point in the curriculum, the teacher can honestly say, "Remember when we learned X and I said we would need it for Y? Well today's the day."

2. Prerequisite Knowledge Is Activated as an Anticipatory Set and So That Misconceptions Can Be Diagnosed

Rollerblades and Conservation of Momentum. In a lesson designed by physics teacher Nicole Robinson,[3] two students were asked to stand on rollerblades facing each other. Before each scenario, students had to write down their prediction of what would happen. For example, "What would happen if only one student on rollerblades pushed and the other did nothing?" Most students responded, contrary to the law of conservation of momentum, that the pushed student would move, while the pusher would remain still.

When the scenario was enacted, of course, both students moved, which students then had to explain. For some students, this provided a chance to activate prior knowledge, which was indeed correct, to apply the appropriate physical law to the situation and perhaps to analyze the task into its relevant and irrelevant components. For other students, the disconfirmation of their prediction presented "a cognitive conflict," the ultimate teachable moment, because students now realize there is something they do not understand.

There are other ways teachers might diagnose which students understand the basics of conservation of momentum (e.g., written cases or scenarios to be considered in a pretest), but there is little doubt that Ms. Robinson's is a clever and dramatic way of gaining students' attention, providing an anticipatory set, and diagnosing whose prior knowledge is accurate and whose is not. She and her students are now ready to address misconceptions and get into the meat of the lesson, other demonstrations and applications, design of additional and more advanced experiments, and the like. Furthermore, if she were to remind students where they had touched on precursors to these ideas in previous science units or classes and when they will see them again in future units, she would have contextualized this lesson as in mastery element #1 above.

Essay Scoring: An Exercise in Unreliability. One of the challenges for instructors in assessment courses or staff development workshops for teachers is to convince them, as Gentile (2000a) stated it,

> Of the difficulty of scoring essays reliably and validly. One can lecture about the problem, discuss the importance of pre-established criteria and rubrics, and even evoke memories of their own perceived horror stories. Still, [they] believe that they somehow will be immune to the problem or that their errors will be insignificant. (p. 210)

As briefly mentioned in the English Language Arts Standards in Chapter 2, Gentile uses some benign deception as an anticipatory set for the topic. At a previous class, students—mostly teachers—are introduced to a set of rules for writing and scoring essay tests and given homework due at the next class to write two essay questions, along with a rubric or scoring key for each question, on the topics they teach. At the beginning of the next class, however, students are divided into groups of three to five and select one of their group to leave the room for a special assignment. After the volunteers leave, Gentile displays an essay question on a topic the class has already discussed, and the remaining student groups are each charged with inventing a key or rubric for scoring the essays the "volunteers" will now be asked to write. At this point, the groups usually breathe a sigh of relief that they don't have to write an answer.

After their scoring-key assignment is clear, Gentile goes to another room where the volunteers have assembled, tells them what their committees of scorers are doing, and enlists them in a ruse. They are all to copy in their own handwriting the same answer to the question. The answer, written by the instructor, includes correct points as well as some inaccuracies.

After about 15 to 20 minutes, when everyone is ready, the examinees turn in their papers and again leave the room while the scorers apply their different scoring schemes and feedback to what they believe to be different essays. After another 10 minutes, when all are done, the examinees return and continuing the ruse, receive their scores and feedback. Then, Gentile asks each examinee to describe to the whole class what score and feedback they received. Finally, one of the examinees exposes the ruse, usually to spontaneous uproar from the class, because the scores assigned range from dismal failure to high pass (from 17% to 100% in four different classes).

All of this exercise constitutes an anticipatory set for the issues of reliability and validity as well as principles of writing essay tests and scoring keys, providing a cognitive conflict and teachable moment that the previous lecture and text could not. Then, these educators reconsider the essay questions and rubrics they wrote for homework.

As in the rollerblade example, there are other ways to activate prior knowledge and diagnose errors—by tests, homework assignments, and so on—but forcing students to confront their own misconceptions via such activities seems preferable. Of course, we still don't know whether students have mastered this new content (which comes in mastery elements #5 and #6), but we are ready for the lesson.

3. Lessons Are Taught Using a Variety Of Methods for Both Basic and Higher-Level Objectives

There is little doubt that teachers are more effective when they have developed a repertoire of teaching methods. A teacher who is proficient using a number of methods can provide variety in instruction (that will likely motivate student learning), is able to satisfy various learning needs at a given point and time, and most important, can attempt to choose an effective method for the instructional goals.

Discovery and Other Teaching Methods. James Lalley (2003) has used the following classroom exercise with preservice and inservice teachers, and it serves as both an anticipatory set and a teaching method.

Students are provided with a class handout describing several teaching methods with examples. They are divided into groups of three or four and instructed to list the strengths and weaknesses/concerns of the various methods, based on their experiences or things they have read. Some strengths of lecturing (direct instruction) that usually arise are that it is efficient in terms of time, can be effective when the lecturer is engaging and fluent in the content presented, and that all students receive the same instruction. Weaknesses include students being relatively passive and there being little formative assessment of student learning in the straight lecture format. Regarding cooperative learning, teachers often mention students learning and practicing social skills and active learning as strengths, and some students relying on others to do the work as well as the increased potential for off-task behavior as weaknesses. Following their work in the groups, the class generates a list of strengths and weaknesses/concerns for each method. In Lalley's words (2003),

> What follows is the most interesting part of the lesson for both the students and the instructor. Because the students have minimally had 12 years of experience in classrooms as students, the majority of them have been exposed to all of the methods and the lists developed for each method are usually comprehensive. Furthermore, the lists of strengths and weaknesses are virtually the same from semester to semester in every class.
>
> Students are then asked to identify which teaching method their instructor was using during this lesson. Students usually respond that it was cooperative learning or discussion. It is acknowledged that there was some cooperation and discussion, but another method best describes the exercise.
>
> At this point, "the light goes on," and students begin to recognize that we were actually doing a form of discovery learning. Students are then asked to describe why this was discovery. The response is usually along the lines of the class having a lot of information about (or experience with) the methods and that the handout provided them a way to structure the information. This is when the distinction between guided and unguided discovery is introduced, and students are asked how we could have done this in an unguided manner. Their response is that we could have openly discussed teaching methods that the students were familiar with, but that the difficulty with that approach was that we would not have been guaranteed as comprehensive a treatment of the topic. At this point, students are told that the lists developed are virtually the same from class to class. The instructor is then in a position to make a critical point and ask the key question of the lesson. He suggests that among other options for teaching this lesson were to lecture about it with a series of overheads or to use the discovery exercise just completed. He then asks the class "If you were to be tested in one week on the content of the lesson, would you have learned and retained more and had higher scores based on a lecture or the exercise?" The response is always unanimous: the exercise.

This teaching methods exercise is not presented to convince the reader that discovery is the best teaching method, although it is often more effective than direct instruction (Hillocks, 1984). Rather, it is a good example of method being well matched to content—a critical component of developing effective instruction. Consider lessons that might be quite inappropriate to teach by discovery: what chemicals should never be mixed, what safety procedures are needed for jumping on a trampoline or using a circular saw, or how to teach a 4-year-old where she lives. Demonstrations, and, yes, even rote memory would likely be ideal choices for these purposes. However, teaching geography by providing students with blank maps and appropriate resource materials or having students work with variations in light, water, and soil content to determine their effects on the growth of plants would be excellent discovery activities. Furthermore, a biology lecture on animals and their habitats presented by an experienced zookeeper would also be effective instruction. It appears obvious, then, that there is no "best" teaching method overall. Rather, different methods are appropriate depending on the content and purposes of instruction, student preparedness, and the teacher's skill with the method. Furthermore, no matter how well done, any method can become habitual, even boring, which will begin to limit its effectiveness. Perhaps Lee J. Cronbach (1966) made the point as well as it can be made:

> I have no faith in any generalization upholding one teaching technique against another. . . . A particular educational tactic is part of an instrumental system; a proper educational design calls upon that tactic at a certain point in time in the sequence, for a certain period of time, following and preceding certain other tactics. No conclusion can be drawn about the tactic considered by itself. (p. 77)

Traveling Like Lewis and Clark via Software. Brenna Towle[4] developed the following ideas for a portion of a 10-lesson unit for elementary social studies. The lesson described here incorporates computer technology as part of a larger professional development school effort (for a description, see Johnson-Gentile, Lonberger, Parana, & West, 2000).

Mrs. Towle described the overall purposes as encompassing two social studies objectives and one technology objective from the New York State Standards:

- Social Studies #1: "to demonstrate their understanding of major ideas, themes, developments, and turning points in the history of the United States."

- Social Studies #3: "to demonstrate their understanding of geography . . . across the nation."
- Mathematics, Science, and Technology #2: "to access and process information using appropriate technologies."

The Louisiana Purchase, the Lewis and Clark expedition, and the resulting western expansion movement were to be explored as some of the specific content of the lessons. Mrs. Towle introduced some of the necessary background by referring to previously studied material and provided some activities to begin the lesson with maps, exploring territorial boundaries, and the like.

Then, using the computer simulation software "The Oregon Trail," students were able to become explorers themselves in the following activities:

1. Students work in groups of four to complete a simulation of a western expedition. Similar to the Lewis and Clark expedition, the setting is the early 1800s, and students begin the lesson by choosing with whom they will travel, when they will leave, and what animals and supplies they will need.

2. As the students travel the trail, they have to determine the pace they will travel, which directly affects their food consumption and the health of the animals drawing their wagons. They will also encounter illness, the impact of wild animals, and the opportunity to trade with locals and natives. They have decisions to make at each juncture.

3. As students travel the trail, they will encounter a number of geographic landmarks, such as lakes, rivers, mountains, and forts. They have to identify these and keep notes in a journal both about the geography and the peoples they encounter.

4. At the conclusion of the simulation, students will reflect on their experiences and choices.

5. For students who complete the simulation before the other students, they can attempt the simulation, again choosing different travel companions, supplies, and so forth.

Out of such experiences come the possibilities for assessing geographical facts about people and places (knowledge level); map-reading skills (comprehension); problem solving, such as distances that can be traveled with certain equipment in a day over various routes (application and analysis); stories to be written and shared (synthesis); and comparisons of routes or decisions in terms of criteria such as safety, supplies, and rate of travel (evaluation). Some of these can be assessed by individual mastery tests and activities, others by team activities as enrichment projects.

The Meaning of the Mean. Among her many suggestions for *The Math We Need to "Know" and "Do,"* Pearl Solomon (2001) has this to say regarding middle-grade treatment of data analysis and its relation to probability:

> An important part of analyzing data sets is to look at how the data are distributed. Understanding distributions helps us make predictions and explain results. We are often interested in where the most events or outcomes are, but looking at the distributions also enables us to consider extremes or outliers less seriously. We also need to consider the range of possibilities.
>
> Stem-and-leaf plots at the early levels can be used with single-variable data. They clearly show where particular values occur most of the time. Early vocabulary development includes the meaning of "the most," "around the middle," "typical," "range," and "average." Later, the terms mean, median, and mode can be related to these from the common vocabulary. (p. 146)

Solomon's outline conforms nicely with the NCTM's (2000) "Data Analysis and Probability" for grades 6-8, but as the standards note, teaching these concepts may be more problematic than is usually recognized:

> In the middle grades, students should learn to use the mean and the mode, to describe the center of a set of data. Although the mean often quickly becomes the method of choice for students when summarizing a data set, their knack for computing the mean does not necessarily correspond to a solid understanding of its meaning or purpose . . . Students need to understand that the mean "evens out" or "balances" a set of data and that the median identifies the "middle" of a data set . . . Thus, the teacher has an important role in providing experiences that help students construct a solid understanding of the mean and its relation to other measures of center. (NCTM, 2000, pp. 250-251)

The number of ways to teach such concepts is probably limited only by the imagination of inventive teachers, but consider the following approaches:

a. What is the same and what is different about each of these distributions of scores from a 10-point quiz?
   (1) 10, 9, 8, 8, 8, 6, 6, 5, 3
   (2) 7, 7, 7, 7, 7, 7, 7, 7, 7
   (3) 10, 10, 10, 8, 7, 6, 4, 4, 4

b. Plot the frequencies of each of these distributions as a bar graph (as done below for distribution 1).

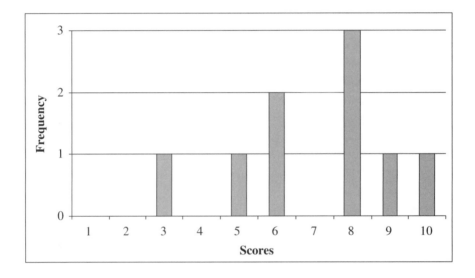

c. Consider the base of the frequency distribution as a number line, plank, or see-saw, and the frequencies as weights. Where would you be able to place a fulcrum to make this see-saw balance?

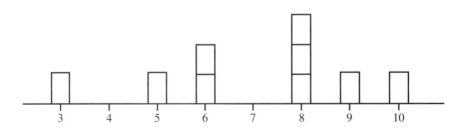

How can you prove it? For example, if the fulcrum is placed at the mean (7) and nowhere else, then the differences between each score and the mean sum to zero (i.e., $3 - 7 = -4, 5 - 7 = -2,$ $2[6 - 7] = 2[-1] = -2$, for a total of -8; while $10 - 7 = 3, 9 - 7 = 2,$ and $3[8 - 7] = 3[1] = 3$, for a total of $+8$; $8 - 8 = 0$).

d. Demonstrate the above on an actual scale or balance beam of your invention so that you can move the fulcrum. For example, weigh 5 or 6 students, have them sit at appropriate distances along a plank marked off as a measured number line, and decide where to place a fulcrum to make the distribution of weights balance.

e. If you wanted to predict the number of points your favorite player or team is likely to score in tomorrow's game, what data do you want to collect to help you decide? Collect such data (from the Internet or newspaper) and compare measures (mean, median, mode) in their predictability over some number of games.

Each of the above suggestions—by no means exhaustive of the possibilities—could be implemented in a variety of ways. For example,

- As a *think-pair-share* exercise, in which students individually come up with ideas, compare their ideas with a partner's, and then share with the class
- As a *cooperative exercise*, with each team learning to do these various approaches to understanding the mean and bonus points (as an enrichment project) awarded to the team when each member of the team passes a subsequent mastery test
- As a brief *lecture/demonstration* by the teacher, followed by students inventing their own problems and teaching them to partners or small groups (*learning by teaching*).
- As a larger scale *inquiry project*, particularly if *a* through *d* are combined, or as *e*

Whatever the teaching method(s) adopted, using a variety of ways of conceiving the mean, comparing it with other measures, and using it in problem solving and problem posing seem essential to truly comprehend it (as the NCTM argued). Fortunately, all of these lend themselves to fairly straightforward criterion-referenced assessments of whether a concept such as the mean can be defined (*knowledge/retrieval*); translated from words to graphs or calculated from actual data *(comprehension)*; transferred to real problems *(application/ utilization)*; compared with other measures in terms of advantages, disadvantages, similarities or differences of meaning, and so on *(analysis)*; and form the basis of creative problems or even test questions *(synthesis)*.

4. Crucial Objectives for Mastery Are Clearly Written and Distributed to Students

Cultural Diversity and Prayer in the Schools. Our Example 2.6 began with the NCSS illustration of Bill Tate's high school discussion on the controversial problem of prayer in the schools. It was illustrative of the standards the NCSS listed under eight "performance expectations for the theme of 'culture,'" three of which are the following (NCSS, 1994, p. xv):

1. Analyze and explain the ways groups, societies, and cultures address human needs and concerns.

2. Demonstrate the value of cultural diversity, as well as cohesion, within and across groups.

3. Construct reasoned judgments about specific cultural responses to persistent human issues.

These are three apparently relevant standards from which one might conclude that the unit on prayer in the schools was derived. On the other hand, there are dozens of other topics that might have been discussed, all perhaps having a claim that they were logically derivative from one of those cultural standards. It is easy to get drawn into debates about how to "design down" from the standards to benchmarks, performance tasks, outcomes and the like (for a comprehensive review of the issues, see Marzano & Kendall, 1996), but we argued earlier that mastery occurs at the classroom level. More will be said about this in Chapter 4. To be even more accurate, mastery learning occurs at the unit level: at the level of Bill Tate's sequence of lessons on diversity and the specific topic of prayer in the schools. It is at that level that mastery objectives are formulated. Based on our analysis of the lesson in Example 2.6 and the surrounding text, we offer the following mastery objectives, formulated as study questions:

1. Describe at least three federal laws or Supreme Court rulings that affect the issue of religious exercises in schools.

2. Are any state or local laws relevant to the issue? If so, describe them in relation to the federal statutes. What are the fundamental similarities? Differences?

3. What constitutional amendments are relevant to the issue of religious exercises in schools? Explain.

4. Compare four or five of the world's religions regarding the following: (a) central beliefs (in two or three sentences), (b) religious holidays and what they commemorate, (c) any beliefs relevant to the issue of religious exercises in schools.

The above four objectives could constitute the required objectives for mastery of a unit—that is, the lowest passing grade. Some of the basic facts of the laws and religions could be tested by objective items on a mastery test, and all could be tested by short essays. Enrichment objectives for more individual study, group projects, or more advanced thinking would also have to be developed (for suggestions, see "A High School Lesson on Diversity," under the NCSS Standards in Chapter 2).

Teaching Creative Writing in Elementary Grades. Consistent with the rubric in Example 2.7 and accompanying text about writing performances, we suggest the kind of mastery objectives that might accompany a creative writing piece. Suppose, for example, that the students were to write about a trip to the zoo or a video about animals one might see in a zoo. Also suppose that the teacher, Ivana Wright, introduces the students to their writing assignment via a "personal analogy" creativity exercise from synectics (Gordon, 1961; Joyce & Weil, 1980): "Pick an animal. What does it feel like to be that animal? How do you relate to the other animals?" Following this class brainstorming activity, students are to select one or two animals and write a creative short story about them, using their best spelling and writing skills. Over the next few days, they would share their drafts of the stories and revise and edit for eventual inclusion in a portfolio.

Given that one cannot have strict mastery objectives for creativity, can mastery learning complement this performance? Yes, in at least two ways. The first is specific to the components of spelling and writing mechanics, which have certain conventional forms that need to be learned. These can be practiced and tested at separate times during the week, parallel to the writing exercise. The second way is more general: Through their prewriting, writing, sharing, and revising, students learn that writing, like any other important skill, is a recursive process in which expertise develops slowly with practice, feedback, more practice, more feedback, and so on.

The following are suggestions for mastery objectives for this exercise, written in the behavioral objectives format that includes behavior, conditions, and format (e.g., Mager, 1962):[5]

1. Following their experiences with zoo animals and other related terminology (e.g., habitat, nocturnal, etc.), students will be able to spell at least 80% of the 30 words on the "zoo list" (distributed to the students) on their mastery tests as well as in their writing assignments.

2. Following their experiences with the zoo animals, as well as the prewriting feedback and first drafts of their stories, students will have no more than 20% errors of the following conventions of writing: (a) capitalization of proper nouns and initial letter of sentences; (b) punctuation, including periods at the ends of declarative sentences, question marks, commas, exclamation points and quotation marks, where appropriate; and (c) grammatical conventions, such as subject-verb agreement.

3. Following their experiences with zoo animals, as well as the prewriting and first drafts and feedback, all vocabulary used will be appropriate and in standard English (unless they purposely violated these standards for effect).

Regarding the creative narratives, no mastery objectives need to be stated (as noted above), but feedback and rewriting for content and style, not just for mechanics, need to be done. If not for grading purposes (see rubric in Example 2.7 for ideas), then reflections and subsequent drafts need to be done for metacognition practice ("Was what I wrote what I intended?"), as well as to encourage creativity ("Can I invent another way of thinking about this?").

5. A Variety of Assessments Are Developed for Mastery Objectives and Enrichment Activities

Throughout this book, we have championed a wide variety of assessments for the many disciplines and levels of schooling that are integral to the standards: from objective tests to essays and performances, from inquiry methods to peer tutoring, from case diagnoses to creative writing and inventing test items, and from laboratory skills to portfolios and self-evaluation. Each of these types of assessment tools has advantages and limitations. To the extent that a testing program relies fundamentally on any one of them alone, teaching as well as learning in that program are likely to be impoverished. Thus good assessment, like good teaching, requires that we use the widest variety of methods as often as possible.

Assessment tools and teaching methods are alike in another way: They require considerable skill to develop and much practice to use effectively. Yet few teachers have had more than a brief exposure to developing tests, performances, rubrics, portfolios, and grading schemes before they are left to their own devices in front of their students. Moreover, the test items that accompany most texts or curricula are often limited to only a few item types or the lowest levels of the Bloom or Marzano taxonomies. For example, as we noted earlier, in one study of more than 10,000 study questions and practice exercises in history and social studies texts, 95% of them were at the knowledge level of Bloom's taxonomy (U.S. Department of Education, 1987, p. 481). Thus learning how to develop classroom assessments remains a prime candidate for continuing professional development programs. It is nevertheless beyond the scope of this book.

What we shall do instead is discuss how a variety of item types can be invented for use—in an overall mastery grading scheme—for both basic mastery objectives and for enrichment activities.

Mastering Spelling via Creative Writing. Building on the example in the previous section, our teacher Ivana Wright included spelling among her mastery goals. Consider some ways of testing for spelling competence, as basic mastery and for enrichment exercises.

a. As a *short-answer item:* The teacher reads the word, provides a sentence for context, rereads the word, and the student writes on the numbered space on the test. Example: the word *habitat.* "We saw the giraffes in their natural habitat." Habitat.

b. As a *true-false item:* Students are to judge whether the underlined word is spelled correctly. If so, circle *T;* if not, circle *F* and correct the spelling. Example: *T* or *F:* "We saw the giraffes in their natural <u>habatat</u>."

c. As a *diagnostic/editing test:* Students read a paragraph and write in the corresponding spaces any corrections needed for the words misspelled on that line. Example:

_____Last week our entire class went to the zoo.

_____Although the monkeys were in cages,

____we saw seven girafs in their

____natural habatat.

d. As a *teaching/tutoring exercise:* Students compile their own lists of words and invent techniques for practicing with a partner and testing each other.

e. As an *enrichment exercise:* Students do exercise *d* as partners, then as 4-person teams. When all members of the team pass the mastery test (e.g., *a-c* above), then all members of the team receive, say, 5 points as an enrichment project.

f. In a *portfolio:* Students maintain two lists of words: those they can spell correctly and those on which they are still working. Every few weeks, they update their lists. In addition, they note in a reflection piece in their portfolios where and how they used the word in one of their creative writings.

It is likely that the vast majority of in-class spelling tests given have been of the short-answer variety in exercise *a*. Such a procedure has the advantages of requiring that students construct answers as well as being efficiently able to test a large number of words in a short time. It has the limitations of being so unique to school that its only likely transfer value is to spelling bees, and it therefore essentially separates spelling from literacy. For variety, if for no other reason, the true-false form is a sensible alternative. Furthermore, note that although two-choice items are usually considered to use the process of selection (or recognition) instead of construction (or recall), requiring corrections blurs that distinction. The remaining examples in the list of exercises bring spelling into the mainstream of literacy. Finally, to show that spelling does not need to be only a knowledge level activity, consider the following examples (which could easily be used as enrichment activities).

g. *Spelling as an analytical essay:* Students are given a word and asked to generate other words that are sounded similarly but spelled differently. Then, they are to invent or reconstruct a rule about the example as well as its exceptions. Or write a song or poem to illustrate the arbitrariness—and fun—of our linguistic exceptions. Example: *Tough, rough,* and *enough* compared with *through* or to *stuff* and *huff.* Any rule? *Receive* and *deceive,* compared with *believe, neighbor,* and *weird.* The rule: *i* before *e* except after *c* or when sounded like *a* as in *neighbor* and *weigh,* or except for weird words such as *weird.*

h. *Spelling as inquiry:* Trace the etymology of a spelling word via the *Oxford English Dictionary,* encyclopedia references, or the Internet.

It should be noted that parallel activities to each of the above can be invented as assessments of punctuation or grammar. The advantages of multiple measures are legion: They elicit thinking at many levels, they use a variety of cognitive processes, they avoid the "one best method" rigidities on the part of teachers and students, and they are in line with the IRA/NCTE standards' emphasis on eclecticism of methods, and therefore the skills and knowledge developed have a higher probability of transferring beyond the classroom to standardized tests as well as to life.

Universal Human Rights. Consider the following unit from the NCSS (1994) standards ("Global Connections": Example #3 for high school):

> In a number of units in her world history course, Glory Ann Fitzpatrick has found that her students become quite agitated by incidents in which rights have been violated. Thus, for a week, Fitzpatrick focuses on the topic of universal human rights by having students reflect on the incidents they have noted and then, in small groups, develop a list of rights they believe all human beings should have, regardless of where they live or their ethnicity, gender, or religion. They bring these back to the larger group and, by consensus, compile a single list from each group's contributions. They then attempt to prioritize these, defining which are essential and non-essential to survival. Students develop written rationales for each right, justifying its inclusion on the list. As a final check, Fitzpatrick asks students to re-evaluate each right in terms of whether it is appropriate across all cultures and time periods they have studied in the course. Where irreconcilable differences among students occur with regard to the universality of the right, students are given the option to present a minority report. She then distributed the Universal Declaration of Human Rights, and has them, working in small groups, compare their work to that of the United Nations. (pp. 137-138)

Ms. Fitzpatrick has certainly devised an exciting unit for her students. It would truly be a shame if the assessment for this unit detracted from that excitement. And yet there are likely some fundamental facts and principles that need to be understood before various governments' policies could be evaluated or effective new ideas proposed. Some of these facts and principles might reasonably be assessed using objective test forms, and others will require essays or reports. Not all need to be required for mastery; some can be enrichment objectives. We offer the following suggestions as a start:

a. As *two-choice items:* Examples of rights can be judged as essential or nonessential in terms of whether they are acknowledged in the United Nation's declaration. Example: The right to a fair wage is _____. *(E or N).*

b. As *short answer items:* Students are given a series of cases or anecdotes, similar to the dilemmas used by Kohlberg (1963) to assess moral development, and have to identify the international right or moral law involved. Example: Drug companies have recently been criticized because the AIDS drugs they produce are too expensive for patients in the Third World. The companies counter that they not only have a responsibility to their stockholders but also that it costs a lot of money to develop and test these drugs. What international law or human right is most fundamental to this case?_____
_____.

c. As *matching* or *multiple-choice items:* The same kinds of cases as mentioned in *b* can be given with selection from four alternatives for each multiple-choice item or with 6 to 10 rights or laws to choose from in the matching format. If matching is used, the instructions should stress that principles can be used once, more than once, or not at all (to avoid one-to-one correspondence between choices and premises and thus control for guessing).

d. As *essay items:* Cases or scenarios can be presented (as in *b* and *c* above) with students required to construct a line of reasoning to be presented by the lawyer for one or both parties to dispute.

e. As *written reports (inquiry projects):* Students are to research a particular incident or conflict, reporting on the historical or cultural roots of the problem; rights or laws involved as well as the legal/moral arguments to be offered by the lawyers for both sides; and a possible resolution to the problem. This could be done as a cooperative team (as Ms. Fitzpatrick has suggested) and used as an enrichment project.

f. As *performances:* Students invent scenarios or dilemmas (such as those described in *b* above) and act them out. These could also be enrichment activities.

g. As a *portfolio:* Students individually collect news items, reflect on them in writing, invent criteria for judging them, and write their own philosophies regarding such issues. Then, periodically through the course, they reflect on these and revise their philosophies.

6. A Plan Is Established for Remediating Any Students Who Fail to Achieve the Required Standards for Mastery

Seasons of the Year and Phases of the Moon. Consider the following two questions:

a. Why do we have seasons of the year?

b. Why are there different phases of the moon?

Common misconceptions for *a* are based on the notion of the earth's greater distance from the sun during winter and for *b* are based on the notion of eclipses putting the moon in the earth's shadow. Such misconceptions occur despite correct instruction and appropriate teacher demonstrations with apparent acquisition by students initially. Nevertheless, this newly acquired information is interpreted in terms of misconceptions students have already acquired; then it is reorganized and reconstructed into sometimes strange amalgams of fact and fiction that the students come to believe is what they were taught. This is not unlike the reconstructive memory processes Bartlett (1932) described or more recent research that Loftus (1992) called "When a Lie Becomes Memory's Truth." Sadly, many teachers have the same misconceptions, as we discuss in Chapter 5.

Regardless of the sources of the misconceptions, it is virtually guaranteed that after initial instruction on such topics, many students will not have mastered the concepts to an acceptable standard. These students will need remedial instruction. One form such remediation might take is to reread the text or repeat the demonstrations and explanations in small groups. Another example, however, is to help the students take responsibility for their own remediation. The NRC standards (1996) suggest that,

Teachers have communicated their assessment practices, their standards for performance, and criteria for evaluation to students when students are able to

- Select a piece of their own work to provide evidence of understanding of a scientific concept, principle, or law or their ability to conduct scientific inquiry.

- Explain orally, in writing, or through illustration how a work sample provides evidence of understanding.
- Critique a sample of their own work using the teacher's standards and criteria for quality.
- Critique the work of other students in constructive ways. (p. 88)

In the "seasons" and "phases" examples above, there seems to be no substitute for students, perhaps all students but especially those in need of remediation, to manipulate objects to demonstrate and explain to themselves and others what is going on. For example, a flashlight or a model of the solar system may be necessary with initial discussions and explorations occurring in groups. But eventually, each student will have to construct and fluently present an explanation.

As noted in mastery element #5, there are many ways to assess most learning. Aspects of seasons of the year or phases of the moon could possibly be assessed by objective test questions, but diagnosis and remediation of students' misconceptions on such questions are probably best assessed on short essays, oral presentations, or one-on-one demonstrations. To score these reliably, an answer key or rubric will need to be available. Most important, given the persistence of our misconceptions and the counterintuitive nature of the scientific explanations, teachers need to be prepared to remediate students who are slow to grasp the concept.

Physical, Artistic, and Mental Skills. When athletes or musicians make an error in one of their actions, remediation is usually a no-brainer: Correct what was wrong and then practice the new skill to the point of overlearning so that it becomes a stronger habit than the older version. This is usually done at first in much the same way that it was initially performed: that is, to keep hitting the same backhand cross court in tennis, playing the sequence of notes or chords in the same musical piece, or trying the triple jump with the same prior movements (and music) in figure skating. When the accuracy of the performance improves and confidence is restored, then we transfer the skill to a new, but similar activity: hitting the backhand down the line, playing a similar music passage in a new piece, or trying the triple jump in combination with another jump. As expertise grows, so does automaticity in recognizing patterns, so that the budding athlete or musician more quickly and fluently identifies what tennis stroke or fingering to use. Even in the fine arts, students spend hours practicing drawings to master individual skills such as shading or perspective.

And yet regarding mental skills, we seem to have the belief as a culture that if you didn't get it at first, trying again is against the rules, unfair to others, or just simply too boring to consider. A teacher example of this was given in IRA/NCTE (1996) Elementary Vignette #7, (in Chapter 2), in which Mrs. D. wanted her students to use various reading strategies and we chided her for having provided neither practice nor assessment. A student example was cited by Garner and Alexander (1989):

> When students in elementary and middle schools notice that they no longer remember information they have read, many do not intentionally reinspect portions of a text that might provide the information. When asked why they do not reinspect texts to find answers to questions, they usually report either that "it is illegal" or that it takes too much time. (pp. 145-146)

It seems apparent that many mental processes have properties that distinguish them from physical or artistic skills. Examples might include the organization and categorization of knowledge, grammatical structures, and recursive processes, as used in writing. Even if this analysis is accurate, and that is by no means certain (e.g., Charness, 1985), there are still many parallels between physical and mental skills regarding the need for a high degree of original learning, practice with feedback, relearning/overlearning, and automaticity. Higher-level intellectual skills, such as reading for comprehension, learning or memory strategies, pattern recognition, mnemonics, classification, metacognition, and writing to clearly say what you mean, not to mention lower-order skills, such as multiplication tables, spelling, punctuation, letter recognition, and phonics, all improve with practice and feedback and do not improve without them.

The conclusion we draw from this, which is reinforced by how the brain learns (see "The Brain Base," in Chapter 1), is that it is not a sin to ask a student who failed to achieve mastery the first time to simply do it again. In fact, our experience with graduate level teachers is that the reasons for most initial failures at mastery tests are twofold: prior misconceptions about the topics and too little preparation or practice for the first test. Thus in requiring that students *do again* what they should have done the first time or just need more time with, we are reinforcing the message they already know from previous experiences in physical domains: To ride a bike, hit a baseball, or ice skate, you have to practice. When we teachers let students off the easy way by passing them on, or even by immediately shifting to an alternative way of demonstrating competence, we are reinforcing the cultural stereotype that you are either smart or you are not.

Having said that, a good mastery program develops a lot of alternative ways of assessing mastery at various levels of thinking, as we have tried to demonstrate. But do not underestimate the power of "If at first you don't succeed, try, try again."

Summary

After showing the complementarity of the national discipline-based standards with state standards, we considered the issues of enrichment and remediation, which are central to the success of both standards and mastery learning. We also emphasized the importance of peer tutoring to help tutors overlearn the material and become metacognitively aware of their learning. Finally, we gave examples from a variety of disciplines and levels of schooling of six elements of mastery learning that are essential for planning lessons:

- That lessons be contextualized in a spiral curriculum
- That prerequisite knowledge is activated (a) as an anticipatory set and (b) so that misconceptions can be diagnosed
- That lessons be taught using a variety of methods, for both basic and higher-level objectives
- That crucial objectives for mastery be clearly written and distributed to students
- That a variety of assessments be developed for mastery objectives as well as for enrichment activities
- That a plan be established for remediating any students who fail to achieve the required standards for mastery

Notes

1. American Association for the Advancement of Science (1993) *Benchmarks for Science Literacy.*

2. Ms. Chilungu, a violinist in the UB Symphony, as well as a graduate student in educational psychology at the State University of New York at Buffalo, provided these firsthand examples for this section.

3. Ms. Robinson invented this procedure to use in her suburban high school physics class. Her description of the problem also shows how our daily experiences often provide interference via misinformation or misperception for scientific concepts.

4. Mrs. Towle was a student teacher under the supervision of Dr. Kay Johnson-Gentile (State University of New York, College at Buffalo) and Joseph Parana (Buffalo Public Schools) when she developed lessons like these specifically to help preservice teachers learn to incorporate technology into their classrooms. See Johnson-Gentile et al. (2000) for a description of this unique program.

5. In this section, we have purposely shown two ways of presenting mastery objectives: as study questions and as behavioral objectives (in the cultural diversity and creative writing examples, respectively). We prefer the former because they are easily shared with students as study aids, but the latter are also appropriate and widely used.

4

Implementing Standards and Mastery Learning in the Classroom

Implementing Mastery Learning: 13 Steps

How and when to begin to convert a course or curriculum to a mastery format may appear to be a formidable task. The good news is that it does not have to be done all at once: You can convert one or two units to mastery this year and add two or three units the following year. Furthermore, not all concepts or units in a curriculum need to be mastered; some units can be deliberately included as creative extensions of the topic, as ways of broadening the curriculum to include fun activities. (In the first published account of an explicit mastery system [Washburne, 1922], mastery objectives were counterbalanced with "social" objectives that were never tested.) Obviously, all this becomes easier yet if you can find a colleague with whom you share both the task and the fruits of your labors: the tests and activities developed.

What follows is a systematic plan for implementing mastery. It includes the major elements of mastery learning, described in the last chapter, but breaks those elements into specific steps or decisions that need to be made based on Gentile (1997) and Block, Efthim, and Burns (1989). Examples are provided from three areas: elementary math, secondary social studies, and an undergraduate teacher education methods course (based on a syllabus invented by Dr. Kay Johnson-Gentile of Buffalo State College).

1. Divide your course or curriculum into meaningful units, perhaps 2 weeks in length. In an elementary math curriculum in which fractions, proportions, and their applications to everyday problem solving are a major focus, two such units might be multiplication and division of fractions. In a secondary social studies course on the U.S. Constitution and Bill of Rights, such a unit might be on prayer in the schools (see Example 2.6 under the National Council for the Social Studies, or NCSS, in Chapter 2 and Element #4 in the previous chapter). In a methods class for prospective teachers, the curriculum might be divided into the following four units: advantages and disadvantages of various teaching techniques, lesson planning, practice teaching, and evaluating instruction.

2. Decide what information and skills are essential for all to master versus what are optional and can therefore be used for enrichment activities (see Step 7).

3. Order the essential information and skills into a logical sequence and write them as study questions or unit objectives (to be distributed to students in the course syllabus or as a handout). In the unit on division of fractions, for example, the following might be study questions for some of the mastery objectives:

   a. In dividing fractions such as 3/8 divided by 1/5, why do we have the rule "Invert then multiply"? Show all steps in the procedure.

   b. How can 3/8 divided by 1/5 be considered the same process as 6 divided by 2? Demonstrate using a diagram and state in words.

Sample study questions for the social studies unit follow (from the previous chapter):

   a. Describe at least three federal laws or Supreme Court rulings that affect the issue of religious exercises in the schools.

   b. Compare four or five of the world's religions regarding the following: central beliefs, religious holidays and what they commemorate, and beliefs relevant to religious exercises in schools.

For the teaching methods course, mastery objectives on the lesson design unit might be as follows:

a. What is the meaning of each component of the lesson plan used by your cooperating school/teacher? Give examples of each.

b. Write a lesson plan that includes each of the components your school requires for a lesson you will later teach.

4. Identify prerequisite knowledge or skills for the mastery objectives (in Steps 2 and 3) so that these can be assessed and, if necessary, retaught prior to beginning the current mastery unit. For the division of fractions unit, prerequisite knowledge probably includes multiplication and division of whole numbers, multiplication of fractions (and processes such as finding the least common denominator), and ways of representing fractions (e.g., as a portion of a whole, as a point on a number line, etc.; see Table 5.1, in Chapter 5).

For the school prayer unit, essential prior knowledge probably means understanding the freedom of religion amendment to the Constitution (First Amendment of the Bill of Rights, established December 15, 1791; see National Archives and Records Administration, 2002) and, perhaps, some of the history of the United States as a safe haven for immigrants who were escaping religious persecution elsewhere.

For lesson planning, knowledge of the instructional components of the plan should probably be assessed. For a Madeline-Hunter-style lesson plan, for instance, students should understand what is meant by *anticipatory set, monitor progress, adjust teaching,* and so forth. For lessons that use cooperative teams, students should know what is meant by *individual accountability* and *positive interdependence,* along with ways to obtain them.

5. Create parallel forms of the mastery test by writing several test questions (three or more) at about the same level of difficulty for each mastery objective. Randomly assign these to different tests to create three or more equally difficult parallel forms of the unit mastery test. Although mastery tests are usually comprised of objective item types such as multiple-choice and short-answer items, it is possible to assess mastery by essays and performances. In these cases, a rubric or scoring key must be devised to enhance objectivity of scoring, and much care must be taken to be sure that the several versions of the assessments are equivalent.

It is important to remember that you are creating a mastery test, not a mystery test. Thus nothing should be tested that was not identified as a unit objective (in Step 3).

6. Establish a passing standard and what grades will be assigned to those who have passed, as well as the consequences of not passing.

  a. Set the standard as high as your capability of test writing and evaluation will allow. In terms of percentage of the items correctly answered, below 75% probably allows chance to play too much of a role (especially with items such as true-false, which have a 50% guessing rate); 100% is probably too high because it requires perfect tests and no error in scoring. Thus, for most tasks, 75% to 90% is probably optimal. Exceptions to this might include safety objectives, such as understanding street signs for young children, using tools and kitchen appliances for older children, and parachute packing for all of us, all of which would require mastery to be set at 100%.

  b. Decide on a policy for what students will need to do if they do not pass, along with what additional help will be available.

  c. Publish the grading policy and your rationale for it (in a syllabus or handout) so students know what you expect.

In the elementary math unit, for example, minimal mastery of the objectives stated in *3a* and *3b* might be set at 80%, since questions to test those concepts can be written at higher as well as lower levels of thinking. (If only the knowledge level were tested, as in testing multiplication tables or following an algorithm, then the passing cutoff might better be 90%.) Achieving 80% or better could earn a grade of *S, C,* or *70* (to accommodate existing grading structures), with the rationale that while demonstrating adequate original learning, even 100% correct on the mastery test is just the beginning, not the end, of learning about this topic (see Step 7 for enrichment exercises to enhance learning, improve retention, and earn higher grades). Achieving less than 80% means the student has not yet passed, as in a driver's test, and must obtain extra help (from peers, parents, aides, or the teacher) and complete certain remedial exercises as a ticket to a retest. Students who cannot eventually pass this test likely need help on prerequisites or are not trying. In either case, they must eventually pass this test to earn credit for this unit or to have any enrichment projects increase their unit grades (e.g., from *C* to *B* or *70* to *80*).

In the social studies unit, a mastery test on objectives *3c* and *3d* would likely be assessing mostly knowledge and comprehension of laws and comparative religious beliefs. Thus it seems quite reasonable that scores of 80% to 100% correct on such items earn a common passing grade of *S, C,* or 70. Below 80% on the test requires remedial activities as a ticket to retest (see Example 2.6). Higher grades, again, are earned by enrichment activities (see Step 7).

In the teaching methods course, minimum passing might have even more extensive requirements. Consider, for example, this statement from the syllabus of Dr. Kay Johnson-Gentile:

> *C* = (1) Pass both course examinations at a mastery level of 80% or better; (2) Satisfactorily complete all homework and in-class assignments; (3) Satisfactorily complete the computer technology laboratory requirement; (4) Create and teach a community building lesson to your elementary class; (5) Hand in all required unit and lesson plans, receiving an overall average of at least 7 points; (6) Receive an acceptable rating on lessons/observations from your professor; (7) Receive an acceptable teaching evaluation from your cooperating teacher (mostly 2's); (8) Demonstrate an ability to work cooperatively with your team members; (9) Write a 1-2 page paper reflecting on your experience in EDU 315; (10) Update your professional portfolio.

7. Create enrichment projects to motivate students to go beyond basic mastery and raise their grades. For the division of fractions unit, peer tutoring should definitely be an available enrichment project. That is, a pupil who demonstrates mastery tutors a peer; when the tutee passes the test, the tutor receives the enrichment bonus. Other enrichment activities might be to invent word problems for formulaic expressions such as 3/8 divided by 1/5; to diagnose errors in case vignettes of students multiplying or dividing fractions; to think aloud when solving problems to self-assess what is easy and what needs more work; to investigate which professions or tasks in the world of work regularly require knowledge of fractions. These tasks tap into the higher levels of Bloom's and Marzano's taxonomies and therefore earn higher grades for the unit (*C* to *B* to *A,* 70 to 80 to 90, etc.), depending on how many are satisfactorily completed. Some, particularly the last, lend themselves to cooperative team projects.

For the social studies unit on prayer in the schools, suggestions for enrichment activities could include dialogical thinking exercises in which students must defend more than one point of view, find or invent win-win solutions to conflicts in the news, and so on. Or similarly, have students find an article about prayer in the news that they disagree with and then have them defend the author's perspective. These tasks extend the cognitive levels beyond those required to pass the test and thus deserve higher grades (as argued in the NCSS lesson in Chapter 2 on "Cultural Diversity" and in Example 2.6).

For the teaching methods course, consider the continuation of Professor Johnson-Gentile's grading policy:

B = (1) Complete all requirements for a grade of C as stated above; (2) Complete the Learning Center Project satisfactorily; (3) Incorporate the use of some type of technology (e.g., overhead, audio or video cassette players, television, filmstrips, slide projector, calculators, etc.) in at least five lessons you teach; (4) Integrate computer technology into at least one of your teaching units; (5) Have an overall average of 8 points or better on lesson plans; (6) Teach at least one lesson to your elementary class independently; (7) Incorporate a class management plan into your teaching; (8) Teach at least one Bio Moment to your class; (9) Conduct at least three class dismissals (with permission and input, of course, from your cooperating teacher); (10) Receive a superior teaching evaluation from your cooperating teacher (mostly 3's), as well as an above average evaluation from your professor.

A = (1) Complete all requirements for a B (as stated above); (2) Work with two students in your elementary class one-on-one to either do remediation or creative extension work on a concept in their math curriculum; (3) Receive the highest evaluation ratings from your cooperating teacher (mostly 4's), as well as the highest evaluation/s from your professor. (Creativity, use of effective teaching strategies, and effective utilization of computer technology must be demonstrated.)

8. Teach to the objectives. If a 2-week unit is planned, use the first week to teach the essential concepts and skills (Step 3) and schedule the initial mastery test on Monday of the second week (for a class that meets daily). As discussed previously, mastery learning is not tied to a particular teaching method; thus you are free to adapt any of the methods our heritage has endowed us with. (Note: This includes the possibility of a totally individualized approach, such as Keller's 1968 Personalized System of Instruction, or PSI, in which students challenge for a test when they are ready. For most school teachers, however, this is too radical a departure, especially if you allow testing at the students' convenience. Thus for most teachers, we recommend that the first mastery test be scheduled for all at the same time, with individualization occurring during the second week.)

9. Optional: Use one of the parallel test forms as a pretest or as a practice test during instruction. Using a parallel test in this manner allows the teacher as well as the students to see their growth and can therefore be motivating and provide direction to the students' studying. Of course, it requires extra forms of the mastery tests.

10. Administer the initial mastery test at the scheduled time. After students take the test, the teacher should score it and review it with students as soon as possible. (Note: This is one of the advantages of objective tests. They can often be scored as students finish so that the test can be reviewed immediately.) The purpose here is to reinforce what students understood and reteach what proved to be misunderstood.

11. Schedule makeup testing at your convenience or during subsequent classes while other students work on enrichment projects. As noted above, students who do not pass must be required to complete remedial activities as a ticket to the next test; otherwise, some students may challenge the limits of your patience and take additional tests without studying. Again, the analogy of the driver's test can be made to the students: If at first you don't succeed, try until you do; until you succeed, no driver's license and no credit for this unit.

During this second week, all students, including those still working to pass the test, may work on enrichment projects or other group-based optional exercises the teacher may devise. The advantages of having enrichment exercises available to all students are at least threefold. First, it avoids some students doing nothing but the basics, while also allowing them to learn material that may help them to pass the test. Second, it provides experiences to all at the higher levels of the Bloom and Marzano taxonomies of thinking. Third, it provides extra incentive to students having trouble with the tests: If they have earned extra points via a successful enrichment project, then passing the test rewards them not only with a passing grade but also with a higher grade.

12. Move on to the next unit. As in Step 4, what happens next depends on whether the last unit was strictly prerequisite to the new one. If it is and some students have not passed the prerequisites, then it is wise to insert another unit into the sequence to give those students more time to catch up. (Note: This is the same problem we have when students were absent from class and missed essential instruction. Sadly, the usual practice is to move on anyway and hope they will catch up. If we do the same thing in a mastery system, we will therefore be no worse than in traditional practice; but we can do better, as suggested here.)

For example, in elementary math, we could do a review of some essentials from a previous year (e.g., addition and subtraction of fractions) or switching to some prerequisites of a later unit (e.g., geometric shapes, angles, and motions, with practice using a computer program such as LOGO). Meanwhile, students who need extra help mastering the required concepts can be provided the help they need. Then, we move on to the next unit in the logical sequence.

In social studies, very few units have logically prerequisite units, and thus it is possible to move from school prayer to a unit on the history of women's rights. Meanwhile, students who did not complete the school prayer unit can continue to work on it in their spare time.

In college classes, as in most of adult life, work does not go away until it is completed. The students will have to complete unfulfilled course requirements on their own time, by mutual agreement with their instructor (or boss). If and when they do, they receive credit for that previous unit. For programs in which certification exists to protect the public, such as teacher certification, passing a course should imply that all required components of that course have been mastered, even if it means postponing graduation.

13. *Devise a way to provide a composite grade for all mastery units.* This should require at least a pass on each unit, with only passing grades to be averaged. For example, if there were three mastery units, then the following average grades might be derived (Note: 80% correct on the test equals C or 70):

	Units 1	2	3	Average Grade
Amy	C	A	B	B
Bill	I	A	A	I
Chuck	70	80	90	80
Delta	60	90	90	0

The point being made here is that until each required unit is mastered, the course cannot be passed. This is parallel, again, with the logic of the driver's test, in which you cannot compensate for a lack of driving skill by a high score on a rules-of-the-road test, or vice versa. Similarly, when evaluating the skills of an automotive technician who had a very high score in the area of steering but a very low score in the area of brakes, we would not average the two and falsely determine that he or she is competent. In both cases, each must be passed independently before you have passed the test.

Summary

Thirteen decisions, or steps, which facilitate converting a curriculum or unit to a mastery format are presented, along with examples from elementary mathematics, secondary social studies, and a teacher education methods course. These constitute a "how-to-do-it" manual designed to complement the more general rationale for mastery learning and the standards presented in previous chapters. Finally, we come back to the common and oft-stated goal of all the standards that might just be realizable through mastery learning, namely, how to really mean it when we say "All children can learn" or "No child left behind."

5

Professional Development and Mastery Learning

The Misadventures of Mastery Learning

John Carroll (1989) related the following discussion he had with a teacher about mastery learning:

> He wanted to consider how one might teach children the meaning of the word musket. Using mastery learning, he thought, he would have to concentrate on teaching the definition of the word, as found in dictionaries, and having children practice writing sentences or stories using the word correctly. In contrast, if he could ignore mastery learning ideas, he would prefer to take the children on a field trip to a museum where they could learn the full meaning of the word by seeing muskets on display and hearing something about their role in the American Revolution. . . .
>
> It is obvious that this teacher, to the extent that he had been exposed to notions about mastery learning, had gotten the impression that it required analyzing learning tasks into small steps and then using drill and practice procedures to pound in the learning. I argued with him, however, that mastery learning, or at least the model of school learning, carries no such implication. The model of school learning requires clear specification of the task to be learned. But this specification need not

break the task into small steps, and it makes no requirement that drill and practice procedures be followed. (p. 28)

Small steps, drill and practice, or a rigid instructional system that allows teachers no creativity on thousands of low-level instructional objectives—this is perhaps the popular view of mastery learning. Marzano and Kendall (1996) describe this view as follows:

> As powerful as the mastery learning model was in some ways, it still required that all units of instruction begin with a formative test, employ correctives and feedback for those students who did not meet the criterion score on the formative test, use enrichment activities for those who did meet the criterion on the test, and so on. (p. 179)

Mastery learning, even in its many varieties, just seemed "too restrictive for teachers who were used to a great deal of academic freedom" (Marzano & Kendall, 1996, p. 179).

Sadly, the implementation of many mastery programs reinforced these stereotypes with list after list of objectives to be mastered, the reinforcement for which was a new list of objectives to be checked off. For the teachers, the goal was to get as many students through as many objectives as possible; thus they felt like testing machines, with little time or energy for creative teaching. And enrichment activities, where there were any at all, devolved into busywork to keep faster learners out of trouble while their slower classmates caught up.

Mastery programs conceived as these small-step programs were soon abandoned, as they should have been. They violated many of the very principles of learning and memory (see Chapter 1), which provided the basis for mastery learning. Compare the following conceptions of mastery learning:

Poorly Implemented	*What Is Needed*
Hundreds of minute objectives per unit	A dozen or two significant objectives per unit
Mastery as completion of a task to be checked off and move on to the next	Mastery as initial learning that will be forgotten and relearned with new examples and in other ways
Enrichment as low-level busywork for fast learners (if at all) while slow learners catch up	Enrichment as higher-level and creative ways to go beyond what was mastered, available to all students

One might lament the bad luck of all of this regarding mastery learning programs, but the more interesting question is whether we have learned anything from these "misadventures of mastery." The recent literature on standards and benchmarks, including a local urban district's recent adoption of them reported in the *Buffalo News*, does not give us much hope that anything was learned.

> When elementary and middle school report cards are mailed this month, parents won't see any grades in math and language arts. Instead, they'll see a list of specific skills in those subject areas and indications of whether their child mastered the skills. If not, there will be suggestions for remediation. . . .
>
> Pupil progress is measured not by a test score, but whether the child has reached a series of benchmarks that clearly demonstrate he or she has mastered a specific skill, such as being able to divide fractions or recognize the parts of speech. (McNeil, 2001, p. A1)

The easiest way to achieve benchmarks, of course, is to sit too long on a bench. And yet, no matter how many benchmarks you attain, a few hours later all traces of them disappear. The analogy to initial learning and forgetting—what we in Chapter 1 called Phase 1 of the learning process—is close to perfect. Thus after all these benchmarks are checked off, students will still forget. Moreover, no one will have gone beyond the levels of knowledge or comprehension on the most basic algorithms or language skills because there is no incentive to teachers or students to do so. We are not against standards and benchmarks, of course, but they must be considered to be only the beginning, not the end. Otherwise, we are seeing the reincarnation of all the worst implementations of mastery: mastery without understanding. It will not be long until these systems, too, are abandoned as being small step, drill and practice, rigid instruction, allowing teachers no creativity on thousands of low-level instructional objectives.

Misinterpretations of Mastery Learning

In an attempt to determine where misinformation about mastery learning originates, Thomas Guskey (1993) examined a number of educational psychology textbooks being used in a preservice teacher education program, to determine the accuracy of information presented about mastery. An examination of 12 of the more prominent textbooks found that only 10 addressed the topic of mastery, and of those 10, the median number of pages devoted to mastery was 2.5, in texts that averaged between 600 and 700 pages—clearly not enough space to describe its philosophical and theoretical underpinnings nor its necessary components. In addition to a less-than-comprehensive treatment of the topic, Guskey identified more disturbing findings:

> Although the vast majority of educational psychology text-books include discussions of mastery learning, our analysis found most of these descriptions to be limited and imprecise. Many, in fact, are conspicuously inaccurate. For example, informed descriptions of mastery learning have consistently emphasized that it is primarily a group-based and teacher-paced approach to instruction, [yet] many textbooks authors erroneously describe it as strictly "individually-based" and "student-paced". . . . One reason for these inaccuracies is likely to be the lack of familiarity among textbook authors with the vast literature on mastery learning. (pp. 9-10)

Guskey (1993) goes on to assert that the underlying cause of such inaccuracies is textbook authors relying on information from existing texts when developing their texts, rather than examining original sources, with fewer than half citing Bloom's (1971) seminal article on the topic. Furthermore, some authors presenting information on the success of mastery often temper it with some erroneous mention of it being limited to lower levels of learning in an attempt to provide a balanced treatment of the topic. According to Guskey, this focus on lower levels of learning runs contrary to empirical evidence:

> Recent research studies show, in fact, that mastery learning is highly effective when instruction focuses on high level outcomes such as problem solving, drawing inferences, and creative expression. (p. 10)

Although preservice teachers have received a less-than-adequate treatment of mastery in most instances, according to Guskey (1993), the results of inservice instruction are more favorable:

> The professional development institutes and staff develop-ment programs focusing on mastery learning generally have maintained integrity to the ideas set forth by Bloom. . . . Mastery learning is generally well received by teachers involved in in-service professional development programs because they readily see its use does not require them to drasti-cally alter what they are doing. Unlike many new ideas and strategies that are designed to replace teachers' current teaching

methods, mastery learning builds upon those techniques. It is seen by many teachers as a means by which they can improve their results with students by making more effective use of skills they already have. (pp. 11-12)

What Is Worth Trying?

We have argued that mastery learning, properly conceived and implemented, will facilitate success of standards in attaining the goals of equity, mastery of basic concepts, problem solving and higher-level thinking, and enthusiastic interest in the subjects studied. The caveat "properly conceived and implemented" implies a mindful and creative application of mastery principles to teachers' content areas so that those teachers can themselves stay enthused about their field, as well as make the kinds of professional decisions that enticed them into teaching in the first place.

Standards can help by providing broad goals—as the National Council of Teachers of Mathematics (NCTM), National Research Council (NRC), National Council for the Social Studies (NCSS), and International Reading Association and the National Council of Teachers of English (IRA/NCTE) documents suggest—but standards also argue that teachers need continuing professional development. We turn to that issue next.

Professional Development of Teachers

NCATE, the Standards, and Teacher Content Preparation

As the major accrediting body for teacher preparation programs, the National Council for Accreditation of Teacher Education (NCATE) has also developed standards, in this case "for colleges and universities that prepare teachers and other professional personnel for work in elementary and secondary schools" (NCATE, 2002, p. 1).

NCATE also concerns itself with educational reform, citing a change in society requiring students to acquire necessary information and develop necessary skills during their school years if they are to be successful later in life. If there are going to be new standards for students, it only follows that there must be comparable new standards for teachers:

Education reform must include the reform of teacher preparation. Reaching the nation's education goals will require high standards for the teaching force. . . . NCATE standards are based on the belief that all children can and should learn. In order to attain this goal, accredited schools, colleges, and departments of education should ensure that new teachers attain the necessary content, pedagogical, and professional knowledge and skills to teach both independently and collaboratively. (NCATE, 2002, p. 3)

NCATE has developed a set of six standards for the development and evaluation of institutions engaged in teacher preparation. Although NCATE primarily discusses "new teachers," it indicates that the standards also apply to advanced programs, which we assume includes programs providing continuing education for those currently teaching.[1] NCATE's standard for "Candidate Performance," the standard that is most closely aligned with the focus of this chapter, states,

Candidates preparing to work in schools as teachers or other professional school personnel know and demonstrate the *content*, pedagogical, and professional knowledge, skills and dispositions necessary to help all students learn. (NCATE, 2002, p. 10; italics added)

It is our belief that one of the strengths of this standard for teacher preparation is that it recognizes the importance of content knowledge for teachers, which is often underestimated and the topic to which now we turn.

Examples From Science and Math

It could be argued that the main reason previous curriculum reforms have failed is that the programs were abandoned before the teachers learned them. For example, the "new math" of the 1970s, with its emphasis on set theory, was quite foreign to students and parents as well as educators, and it took a major reeducation of teachers to understand, let alone teach it. The current math and science standards recognize that staff development is essential for effective implementation of their respective standards, but the problem is formidable—much more formidable than they acknowledge.

Consider the NRC (1996) document, which has three sets of "Professional Development Standards" for teachers of science—to be clear, this means all teachers, because the content standards begin in kindergarten. The document outlines that professional development for teachers of science requires the following:

a. "Science content through the perspectives and methods of inquiry" (p. 59). This includes experiences in actively investigating significant phenomena scientifically; becoming familiar with the literature, media, and technology that can allow lifelong pursuits; building on current understandings; and doing all of this through inquiry methods (as defined above) and in collaboration with the other teachers.

b. "Integrating knowledge of science, learning, pedagogy, students; it also requires applying that knowledge to science teaching" (p. 62). This includes doing everything in *a* and using these ideas in teaching science lessons to students varying in backgrounds, interests, and rates of learning.

c. "Building lifelong understanding and ability for lifelong learning" (p. 68). This includes opportunities to teach, reflect, receive coaching/mentoring, and have access to scientific knowledge, as well as opportunities to help generate it.

Given this rather comprehensive set of standards, why, then, did we introduce them with the comment that the problem is more formidable than the NRC acknowledges? Because nowhere do they face the fact that current teacher knowledge and scientific inquiry ability is like that of the general population: entirely unsatisfactory and mostly misinformed. The exceptions might be high school science teachers, who have at least majored in a scientific discipline. Thus where Standard A suggests that professional development needs to "build on current knowledge," that is a considerable understatement, most likely made so as not to offend teachers. But to fix the problem of science or math literacy for all, we must recognize that the vast majority of teachers—and perhaps teacher educators—cannot at present meet the content or inquiry standards proposed. Consider the following two illustrations of the problems: one from elementary math and the other from elementary science.

Representing and Dividing Fractions

The first illustration, based on the NCTM standards, was presented in Table 2.1. The two questions, about representing and multiplying fractions, respectively, were presented as a pretest exercise to

Table 5.1   What Do Educators Know About Fractions?

	Frequency	
Item	*Number Attempted*	*Correct*
1. Demonstrate at least the following ways to represent (or teach) the fraction 3/8:		
a. As a portion of a whole	28	27
b. As a quotient	23	11
c. As a point on a number line	27	19
d. In some other way of your invention	12	12
2. Demonstrate at least two ways that show why 4/5 divided by 3/8 equals 2.13. Suggestions:		
a. $4/5 \div 3/8 = 4/5 \times 8/3 = 2.13$	20	12
b. $4/5 = .8$ and $3/8 = .375$, so $.8 \div .375 = 2.13$	8	8
c. $4/5 \div 3/8 = 32/40$ divided by $15/40 = 32/40 \times 40/15 = 2.13$	2	1
d. Bars or pies	3	0

the senior author's master's level summer class on the psychology of learning and instruction. In this class of 29, 18 identified themselves as teachers (English, reading, elementary education, early childhood, or English as a second language), 4 as school counselors, 2 as librarians, 1 in communication disorders, 1 as a counseling psychologist (with a PhD working on a state license), and 3 who did not identify their field. Their results on the questions are presented in Table 5.1.

Of the 29, only 5 (17%) correctly identified four ways to represent the fraction 3/8; an additional 10 (34%) could do three of four; 8 (28%) could do two; 5 could do one; and 1 got no correct answers. Regarding the specific solutions, 28 of the 29 represented 3/8 as a fraction of a whole, usually by a pie or bar with shading for three of the eight segments.

As a quotient, the answer was scored correct only if it was clear that 3 needed to be divided by 8 to obtain .375 (writing "three eighths" as 3/8 was not given credit). Of the 29, 6 left it blank, and of the rest, only 11 answered it fully.

Representing 3/8 on a number line was attempted by 27 educators, 19 (70%) of whom correctly showed it as a point between zero and one. The 8 others who attempted it failed because their number line went from 1 to 8, with 3 circled or marked in some way.

Only 12 persons (41%) attempted a fourth way to represent the fraction, usually via a drawing, and they were all credited with a sensible solution. One teacher cleverly expressed her feelings about the task by drawing three happy faces next to five unhappy faces, with the caption "3/8 are happy about math (and I'm not one of them!)."

Regarding Item 2, only 6 of 29 (21%) were able to devise two correct ways to demonstrate that 4/5 ÷ 3/8 = 2.13. Seventeen (59%) were able to demonstrate one way, while 6 others were unable to solve the problem in any way.

The approaches, shown at the bottom of Table 5.1, show that 33 solutions were attempted by the 29 educators, only 21 of which were correct. None of the three visual/graphic solutions attempted were complete or correct. Clearly, these educators have an algorithm-dominated mentality about such problems (as Madeline Hunter quipped, "Ours is not to wonder why; just invert and multiply") which, when they can recall it, mostly works. But even when their recall of the algorithm is high enough to solve the problem, their understanding is significantly below the NCTM standards for teachers (if not for students). See Note 2, page 81, for other solutions.

Seasons of the Year and Phases of the Moon

The second illustration was inspired by the Merrill Education Video titled *A Private Universe* (Scheps & Sadler, 1985). The video begins by asking graduating seniors, and some professors, at a Harvard University graduation to explain (a) why we have seasons of the year and (b) why there are different phases of the moon. The results are embarrassing, not just because the vast majority of the interviewees cannot answer correctly but also because they are not conflicted about their incorrect understanding; rather, they confidently explain their unsupportable assertions. (Perhaps this is the main value of higher education: One gains the bravado to muddle through despite ignorance).

The video then takes us to a high school class in which the Harvard results, not surprisingly, are replicated (but without as much evident self-confidence). Most important, the results are interpreted as showing the power of our preconceived notions. Even when students learn a correct explanation, they often persist in constructing their new understanding on the scaffold of their previous beliefs, with bizarre results. One top-of-the-class student, for example, after learning that the seasons were caused by the 20-some degree tilt of the earth's axis, combined that with her previous explanation of direct and indirect sun's rays (i.e., during winter the sun's rays arrive indirectly by reflecting off something in the cosmos).

So how would teachers do on such questions? In the spring semester of the same course described in the previous section, 38 master's level students were asked to write answers and provide illustrative diagrams to the two questions. Following that, we viewed the video and discussed the implications in terms of constructivist theory and memory research. Of the 38 students, 5 explained the seasons correctly, and 3 were competent regarding lunar phases. Only 3 students explained both correctly. Giving credit for any portion of their answer that was correct (e.g., "The moon is seen in whole or in 'slices' based on its position around the earth"), partial credit would have been received by 9 and 6 persons for the seasons and lunar phases questions, respectively.

The most common misexplanation for the seasons, presented by 9 persons (24%), was based on distance (e.g., "for about 6 months we are closer to the sun, and for 6 months we are farther away"). Regarding lunar phases, the most common misunderstanding involved eclipses: 13 persons (34%) suggested the moon was in the earth's shadow, while an additional 2 persons (5%) argued—believe it or not—that the sun cast the shadows responsible for the moon's visible shapes.

Clearly the majority of educators in the previous demonstrations lack the necessary content knowledge to teach about dividing fractions or the earth's seasons. Given that the participants would all be considered to be well-educated people, let's consider in terms of the learning process why many lacked the requisite knowledge to teach such lessons (even though some were likely certified to do so).

- What was needed to do the fraction's task or understand the season's concept was never taught to the participants.
- What was needed to do the task or understand the concept was covered in class but never learned.
- Participants may at some point have learned the task or understood the concept to some degree but not to an acceptable level of basic understanding.
- Participants may have learned to an acceptable level of understanding but were provided with no opportunity for enrichment and/or overlearning, including the opportunity to learn it by teaching it.

- Participants may have developed a basic fundamental understanding, with some opportunity for overlearning and/or enrichment; however, the content was not embedded in a spiral curriculum and revisited with other applications or for other analytical reasons.
- Acceptable forms of initial learning, possibly with some overlearning, occurred. However, their professors and supervisors in their teacher education programs may have assumed they understood such concepts instead of assessing it and reteaching if necessary.

Recommendations for Staff Development

As was noted by Guskey (1993), staff development on mastery learning has been successful. However, staff development on mastery learning alone is likely to bring about little change in teaching and student achievement. At least this will be the case if mastery learning is presented in the limited workshop format that typifies staff development, in which teachers learn about some innovation outside of the context of what they are teaching in their classrooms and are left to do the implementation on their own. Joyce and Showers (1995), who have conducted extensive analyses and syntheses of research on staff development, report that *successful staff development efforts share the following characteristics:*

1. *Content.* First, these programs all focused on content in curriculum, instruction, and technology. As near as we can tell, only content dealing with curriculum, instruction, technology, or the overall social climate of the schools is likely to improve student learning.

2. *Implementation.* Content of the highest quality will not change student learning unless it is implemented. All these programs developed adequate training, and they organized the teachers and administrators to implement the content of the programs.

3. *Inclusion.* The programs . . . involved all the teachers and administrators in particular schools or, in some cases, all the personnel in the school districts where they took place. . . . There are reports of individual teachers and small groups who have made salutary progress, but translating changes in one or a few classrooms into an effect on the entire student body has not been reported.

4. *Goals and Inquiry.* Finally, goals and the understanding about how to achieve them were kept central. For example,

- All have had specific student-learning goals in mind. None have had only general goals of the "to make the test scores go up" variety.
- All have measured learning outcomes on a formative and summative basis, collecting information about student gains on a regular basis rather than leaving evaluation to a yearly examination of post hoc information derived from standard tests only.
- All have employed substantial amounts of staff development in recognition that the initiative involved teacher and student learning of new procedures. The staff development targeted the content of the initiatives specifically. Data about the progress of implementation were collected regularly and made available to project personnel. (pp. 55-56)

Furthermore, staff development can only be said to be successful to the extent that it positively affects student achievement. These qualities are representative of changes in the prevailing wisdom regarding staff development. According to Hawley and Valli (1999), there has been a paradigm shift in recent years. Central to this shift is the notion that schools should no longer be viewed only as places where teachers teach but also places where teachers learn.

In the old paradigm, in-service workshops emphasize private, individual activity and are brief, often one-shot sessions; offer unrelated topics; rely on an external "expert" presenter; expect passive teacher-listeners; emphasize skill development; are atheoretical; and expect quick visible results. In contrast, in the new paradigm staff development is a shared, public process; promotes sustained interactions; emphasizes substantive, school-related issues; relies on internal expertise; expects teachers to be active participants; emphasizes the why as well as the how of teaching; articulates a theoretical research base; and anticipates lasting change will be a slow process. (Hawley & Valli, 1999, p. 134)

Inherent in this slow process, similar to students meeting learning standards, is that for effective learning to occur through staff development, teachers must have initial instruction, have the opportunity to transfer what was learned to their classrooms, and receive feedback about this implementation. Furthermore, we agree with Hawley and Valli (1999) that if staff development does not have the new characteristics listed above, not only will current efforts be futile but there will also be a negative impact on those teachers experiencing ineffective instruction:

> As what is learned from professional development is implemented, learners often discover what they need to be effective. If that need for learning, resources, and support is not met, increased professional competence and student achievement are unlikely to be experienced and the motivation to engage in additional professional development will be affected. (pp. 140-141)

Consistent in all the current literature on staff development is the notion that it is viewed as an active learning process with opportunities for practice and feedback. Furthermore, to be effective, staff development must focus on the content that teachers teach, requiring teachers to further develop their content knowledge and to think about what they teach at more complex and abstract levels, with the intent of nurturing the same levels of thinking in their students.

Teacher Perceptions of Staff Development

Garet, Porter, Desimone, Birman, and Yoon (2001) conducted a large-scale survey of math and science teachers receiving staff development instruction as part of the nationally funded Eisenhower Staff Development Program. They received responses from 1,027 teachers regarding teachers' perceptions of what is effective in staff development. They identified characteristics of staff development that teachers report as increasing their knowledge and skills in the areas in which they teach, as well as affecting positive change in classroom practice. Teachers report that key components are a focus on content learning, opportunities for active learning, and coherence with other learning activities. They also report that the opportunity to work with other teachers, preferably from the same school, in study groups is effective and that for development to be effective, it must be sustained over a considerable period of time. They also note that mentoring and coaching, in addition to teacher study groups, are effective when they occur during school, which provides an authentic context for practice and problem solving. This leads to these teachers planning how the new curriculum will be implemented. Eventually, these teachers will be involved in presenting this information to other teachers, leading staff development efforts, and developing written materials.

Links to Mastery

One cannot help but notice the links between professional development described in this chapter and the fundamentals of mastery learning discussed throughout this text. In other words, the learning process we describe for students is *identical* to that for teachers. To be effective, staff development must have the following characteristics:

1. Provide opportunities for active rather than passive learning

2. Provide opportunities for practice and subsequent feedback

3. Focus on content and allow/require teachers to think at increasingly higher levels of cognitive complexity

4. Be sustained over a period of time to allow concepts and content to be revisited following some opportunity for reflection and perhaps in a new context

5. Eventually allow teachers to be leaders in staff development, including the development of learning materials for teachers and students

These items mirror the process of learning as discussed when describing students: Allow the learner to be active, provide practice and feedback, design instruction that requires students to think at higher levels, revisit concepts to allow for overlearning, and allow students the opportunity to teach what was learned to others (i.e., peer tutor). Furthermore, although teacher study groups were not described in detail, we can safely assume that these interactive groups also allowed for teaching to others (which undoubtedly resulted in better understanding), feedback, practice, and so on.

Teacher Knowledge

As the preceding sections portray, good teaching involves a complex mixture of talents and domains of knowledge. In Lee Shulman's (1986) classification, teachers need to have knowledge in four domains, three of which are integral to the content they teach, while the fourth is generalizable to teaching in most fields:

- *Subject-matter content knowledge.* What the teacher understands and can do in the discipline he or she teaches: math, chemistry, French, anthropology, art, physical education, and so on.

- *Curricular knowledge.* What the teacher knows of the various materials available to study the content and procedures of the discipline: texts, software, videos, laboratory manuals or simulations, Web sites, and so on.

- *Subject-matter pedagogical knowledge.* The repertoire of skills the teacher has for representing the ideas and content of the discipline to students at various ages and levels of experience: the ability to diagnose students' misconceptions about fractions or phases of the moon, for example, and to devise ways to teach and assess their students' progress.

- *Pedagogical knowledge of teaching.* The generic body of knowledge and repertoire of skills teachers possess regarding instructional and assessment methods: stages of development; principles of learning, memory, and transfer; techniques for classroom management; communication skills; how to give a good lecture, conducting cooperative groups, inventing inquiry lessons; writing tests or rubrics; and using mastery learning procedures.

Shulman (1986) closed his presentation on teacher knowledge with a cute but profound amendment to George Bernard Shaw's infamous aphorism:

Those who can, do. Those who understand, teach. (p. 14)

Teachers need to be expert in their field, yes, but what separates them from "mere experts" is that teachers also need to be expert in teaching: by being conscious of the steps needed to progress from novice to expert, by being able to diagnose what different students need, and having a large repertoire of techniques to achieve instructional goals and maintain the patience necessary to persevere when some students are lost. After all, as John Holt (1964) stated it, "To rescue a man lost in the woods, you must get to where he is" (p. 103).

Teaching, by all these accounts, is a daunting task. It is not for the faint of heart to enter a career in which one must be a content expert, a diagnostician, a rescuer, a patient communicator, a manager and leader, a student of human behavior, and on and on. Moreover, we embark on this task, if Erikson's (1963) theory is even partially correct, long before we have reached the developmental stage (middle age) in which we are ready to teach, by virtue of having resolved our own earlier developmental crises.

Thus when the various standards documents and other observers, including us, contend that teachers need better initial preparation or continuing professional development, we should remind ourselves to do so with great respect. One way to demonstrate such respect is through professional development programs that practice what they preach by being themselves firmly grounded in the content and teaching principles we want the teachers to learn about and use. Professional development programs should therefore include at least the following components (e.g., Gentile, 1997; Joyce, Hersh, & McKibbin, 1983):

1. New material needs to be initially learned to a high level.

2. Teachers must learn the principles on which new techniques or content are based. (No longer can we say, "Just tell me what to do." We need to know why we are doing it.)

3. Teachers need to see exemplars of good techniques and practice the techniques with feedback and coaching.

4. Practice must be distributed in time to provide overlearning.

5. Practice must include multiple ways to solve or pose problems or use a technique to avoid the "one best method" mentality.

6. Practice, with coaching, should be provided in the target situations (grade levels, schools, subjects, etc.) in which teachers are expected to use the new knowledge or skill.

7. Opportunities for reflecting on the new ideas or practices need to be provided.

8. Collaboration needs to be established with other teachers at different grade levels within the spiral curriculum, as well as at the same grade level (which is the usual practice).

Mastery Learning: A Plan for Action and a Professional Development Agenda

We have argued throughout this book that the current standards movement will fail until and unless it incorporates what has been learned about mastery learning. Our objective was to provide the philosophical and theoretical bases for mastery, to enunciate the misconceptions or poor practices associated with mastery learning, and finally to demonstrate alternative ways to implement mastery principles and procedures in a variety of fields and grade levels. We close this chapter with a summary of those principles and procedures, which we believe can serve as both an agenda for mastering mastery learning as well as for successfully implementing the standards, thus making a virtue out of necessity.

Grading

We begin with grading, which for most programs, including mastery programs, is an afterthought. Grades and the assessments from which they arise, however, are the prime motivators for what and how students study. This is true whether or not teachers intend it. Furthermore, the entire purpose for mastery learning can be subverted by a grading system which, for example, is competitive among students in the class (i.e., norm referenced), adds points for attendance or effort, rewards initial learning with the highest grades, or gives only partial credit for second or third chances.

A logical mastery grading scheme must have all three of the following components:

1. *It must be criterion referenced.* This implies, first, that the domains of essential knowledges and skills to be learned are clearly specified (via study questions, objectives, or benchmarks) and second, that students are assessed in relation to how adequately they have acquired those basics (independently of how well other students have performed). The judgments to be made are *OK* vs. *Not OK,* *Mastery* vs. *Nonmastery,* or *Pass* vs. *Incomplete* or *Not Yet Pass,* as in a driver's test.

2. *It must assign the lowest passing grade to initial mastery of the essential knowledges and skills even if the student scores 100% correct on the test.* The rationale for this can be stated as follows: "Congratulations. You've learned the basics and are now ready to begin to use this knowledge or skill." Just as all people get the same driver's license, whether they just passed or "maxed' the test, this is all initial acquisition implies for most tasks (see the exception below). After all, the learning/memory curves demonstrate that initial learning will only be forgotten and must therefore be conceptualized as a means to a larger end: relearning, overlearning, reconceptualization,

automatization, and so on. The only exception to this is for quite complex tasks such as inquiry or writing projects, which require a rubric (as in Examples 2.2, 2.4, 2.5, and 2.7). Thus the lowest passing grade must be defined as S (*Satisfactory*), 75, or C.

3. *It must provide higher grades for satisfactory enrichment projects.* Students should know that they can achieve higher grades by applying their knowledge or skills in various ways: demonstrating greater fluency or automaticity, teaching others, cooperating with a team on a creative production, or independent study. These are optional projects that reinforce and apply the basic concepts or skills that were tested for mastery but at higher levels of thinking. Because they are optional, students who do them are demonstrating motivation, and thus no extra credit need be given for effort. Enrichment projects could be available at any time even before the unit is mastered, because they can help answer the question students often have: "Why do we have to learn this stuff anyway?" Grading of enrichment projects can be *OK* or *Not OK*, with feedback and the opportunity to remediate an unacceptable project until it is acceptable. When it is *OK*, it earns additional points (e.g., 5 or 10) or a higher grade (e.g., the unit grade increases from C to B). Team projects earn the bonus for all team members.

The above grading system is consistent with the mastery philosophy and the learning memory principles on which it is based. Interestingly, it still tends to produce a distribution of grades, though not a normal distribution. This is because unit grades can be averaged as long as a student has achieved mastery on each unit. For such a student, a C, B, and A averages to a B; or a 75, 95, and 85 averages to an 85. For a student who did not master one of the units, however, the course grade is *Incomplete (I)* until at least basic mastery is achieved on that unit. Thus a student with grades I, B, and A cannot yet get credit for the course. This, of course, is what happens if you pass the performance component of the driver's test but not the written portion, or vice versa: No driver's license is given until competence is demonstrated on both components. Table 5.2 illustrates these processes.

The mastery learning literature is not consistent regarding these recommended procedures, likely because grading has been mostly an afterthought. Consider the following change of opinion by some of the most prolific supporters of mastery learning:

Table 5.2   How Course Grades Are Derived From Mastery Units According to the Text

	Unit 1	*Unit 2*	*Unit 3*	*Course Grade*
Stephanie	B	C	A	B
Malcolm	B	I	A	I
Sergio	75	95	85	85
Selena	60	95	85	0

In the strictest interpretation of mastery learning, students have either mastered the course goals or they have not. We know, however, that some students have mastered some of the goals and some have not. What can we do with these students? Two options seem available. First, course grades can be assigned based on the number of course goals mastered. That is, 90% of goals mastered equals an A, 80% a B, and so on. In point of fact, this approach was initially preferred (Block & Anderson, 1975). We now prefer the second option, namely assigning "incompletes" to students who fail to achieve mastery. (Block, Efthim & Burns, 1989, p. 215)

In other words, although there are other ways of making mastery learning compatible with traditional grading, compromising on the above three points undermines the benefits of mastery learning.

As a final point concerning grading, it will be noticed that mastery grading provides little useful data for *norm-referenced purposes,* such as rank in class. One can always give a test and derive both criterion-referenced and norm-referenced scores from it (e.g., 80% = *Pass;* and if the mean and the standard deviation were 75 and 5 respectively, a score of 80 is also at the 84th percentile), but criterion-referenced tests typically do not provide a sufficient range or variability to provide reliable norm-referenced rankings. Thus the best procedure for obtaining ranks is to develop or adapt a test for that purpose. Fortunately, that is what standardized tests do well, and most of them can provide norm-referenced information using national, state, regional, or local norms.

Much more could be said on these topics, but we shall have to leave the reader to search out other references (e.g., Block et al., 1989; Gentile, 1997). In any case, your mastery grading scheme will have to be adapted to your discipline and purposes, as noted specifically in Examples 2.2 through 2.9 and throughout this book.

Selecting Mastery and Enrichment Objectives

Having arrived at a plan for grading that will work for your course, the next step is to decide specifically which objectives and activities must be mastered and which can be optional or enrichment. *Mastery objectives* should be a relatively small number of significant concepts, procedures, and thinking strategies for a unit of instruction that are essential to understanding the topics being studied. The standards of each discipline can help decide what those should be (as illustrated in Chapter 2), but there are two surefire ways of deciding:

1. Do these mastery objectives fulfill goals from previous units (in the spiral curriculum) when we promised, "You will need this later when we study ____"?

2. Are these concepts, knowledges, skills, or thinking strategies prerequisite for subsequent concepts later in the course (or the spiral curriculum)?

If the answer to either of these questions is "yes," then this concept needs to be mastered. If the answer is "no" or "maybe," then the objectives can be part of an *enrichment exercise,* either (a) to be selected as an optional project by those who find it interesting or who are ready for it (and thus get bonus credit above the basic mastery grade, as described above) or (b) to be experienced by all as a social activity or a chance for the teacher to model his or her concern or excitement about a concept, its applications, or its ethical dimensions (and thus likely not graded at all).

Note, as we argued earlier, that if mastery learning is conceived solely as achieving benchmarks, one after another, then any level of excitement the teacher has for teaching the subject will atrophy. Having enrichment activities for each unit—perhaps at least half of each unit—is not just useful for enabling students to go beyond mastery, it maintains the sanity and encourages the creativity of teachers.

Assessing Mastery

The most difficult part of mastery learning, at least initially, is developing the assessments. *Mastery tests must be developed before the course begins* because you need several parallel forms of each test or exercise. To write four parallel forms of a multiple-choice test for a unit with 20 mastery objectives, for example, you need to write four items to test understanding of each of the objectives. Each of these items can then be randomly assigned to one of four forms (A, B, C or D) of 20 items each. If some items test more than one objective, then you do not need one item per objective, but *the crucial point is that the tests must be parallel in content coverage and difficulty.* If you write one form of a test and after administering it decide you need another form for tomorrow, it is virtually guaranteed that the second test will not be parallel.

The same is true for essays or performance tests. They may seem easier and quicker to write, but it is just as hard to make them parallel in content and difficulty, and writing a rubric for scoring them in parallel fashion adds an additional obstacle.

An unexpected benefit of devising your mastery assessment before the course begins is that you will likely discover several objectives for which you cannot invent test questions or rubrics. To borrow from a famous line (from the movie, *Field of Dreams*), *if you cannot build it they will not come*—in this case, come to master it. We suggest shifting objective from the mastery list to the enrichment list.

Assessing Enrichment

Although it is possible to assess some enrichment projects with rubrics, especially extended inquiry or writing projects, most can be assessed by a simple *OK* or *Not OK*, with feedback. Projects that meet the criteria, which must be made available in writing as part of the instructions or contract, are approved and earn the bonus points. For example, tutoring projects may be *OKed* when the tutee passes a parallel form of the mastery test on that unit, or a writing project may be *OKed* when it is mechanically and grammatically correct and shows the kind of creative work specified in the project.

When a project is *not yet OK*, the student must act on the feedback provided and can resubmit until it is *OK*.

Teaching for Mastery: All Children Can Learn

As stressed by every standards document as well as every model of instruction, mastery learning advocates no particular teaching method. Rather, the widest variety of methods are encouraged—from direct instruction to discovery, from cooperative to individual, from occasional drill-and-practice to occasional creative problem posing, from demonstrations to drama, and from paper-and-pencil to technological exercises. *The goal is both simple and profound: for the teacher to do whatever is necessary to induce each student to do whatever is necessary and persevere long enough both to learn the content and demonstrate that learning.*

Once the grading system is in place, the unit's mastery objectives are handed out as study guides, the mastery assessments have been developed in parallel forms, and the enrichment activities are ready, all that needs to happen is to teach that unit. This includes, of course, remedial activities. Far from cramping a teacher's style or limiting what the teacher can do, experienced mastery instructors find that all those preparations free them to concentrate on each student and on the content. These are the reasons teachers chose their profession in the first place: because they want to work with children and/or they love their discipline. As they see "all our children learning" (to cite Benjamin Bloom's 1981 book title), they will have renewed excitement about teaching because they will start to believe what the standards proclaim: All children *can* learn.

Standards advocates, by adopting mastery principles, may even come to believe it, too. So let's close with one of the statements by Bloom (1968) that recruited advocates to mastery in the first place.

> Can all students learn a given task to the same high level of complexity? Studies of aptitude distributions in relation to student performance indicate that there are differences between the extreme (1 to 5 percent at each end of the scale) students and the remainder of the population. At the top of the aptitude distribution, there are likely to be some students who have a special talent for the subject. At the bottom, there are individuals with special disabilities for particular subjects. In between, however, are approximately 90 percent of the students for whom we believe aptitudes are predictive of rate of learning rather than level or complexity of learning possible. Thus, we propose that 95 percent of the students (the top 5 percent plus the next 90 percent) can learn a subject to a high level of mastery (for example, an *A* grade) if given sufficient learning time and appropriate types of help. (p. 5)

Summary

Mastery learning has seen its share of misadventures, most notably being concerned primarily as a small-step, drill-and-practice system for achieving basic low-level objectives. Sadly, the current standards movement appears to use benchmarks in that same limited way, thus being destined to repeating the historical errors instead of learning from those errors. Not surprisingly, these misconceptions parallel difficulties with previous reforms in education as well as new learnings (by both teachers and students) that attempt to correct errors of understanding in math or science. Properly conceived, mastery learning is not only new content to many teachers but can also be the vehicle for appropriate staff development programs in general. That is, staff development programs need to assure that teachers (a) learn new material to a high level, (b) learn both "how to do it" and the principles on which those practices are based, (c) see exemplary models and then practice with feedback and coaching, (d) practice for overlearning and multiple ways of approaching problems in target situations, and (e) reflect on the ideas and collaborate with others who teach in the spiral curriculum. Finally, essentials of mastery learning are reconsidered: grading and selecting and assessing mastery and enrichment objectives.

Note

1. The National Staff Development Program (NSDC, 2001) has also developed standards for teacher education—in this case, for inservice teachers' continuing development—that are less detailed but similar in intent to the NCATE standards described here.

Appendix

What Does the Literature Tell Us?

Two Approaches to Mastery Learning

Hundreds of empirical studies have compared mastery learning methods with one or more traditional methods, spanning the range from elementary school to graduate school in just about every subject area. As briefly outlined in Chapter 1, most of these studies can be clearly categorized into two types of mastery learning, both of which usually trace their lineage to seminal papers published in 1968, as follows:

- *Learning for Mastery (LFM)*, based on Benjamin Bloom's interpretations and adaptations of John Carroll's model of school learning, in which initial instruction is provided through a variety of methods to the whole class, with individualized instruction provided as needed following a mastery test.

- *Personalized System of Instruction (PSI)*, based on Fred S. Keller's ideas, in which individualized instruction is provided for all phases of learning, with occasional large-group exercises, such as lectures, scheduled as reinforcers for those who passed the mastery test (and are therefore presumably prepared for it).

To provide individualized instruction, PSI identifies "proctors" to serve as peer tutors for each student. These proctors are students who have passed the course or unit and receive additional credits for helping their tutors pass the test, while simultaneously learning the material better themselves. This arrangement, most often conducted at the college level, allows for individualized instruction with very large classes (with many proctors each assisting, say, 10 to 15 enrolled students in mostly one-on-one instruction as needed). The course instructor, meanwhile, rotates through the classroom, consulting with proctors and students to facilitate their learning and to provide occasional lectures/demonstrations (for those who are ready for them).

LFM classrooms tend to resemble more traditional instructional arrangements, with the teacher up front and central in directing activities, whether they be lectures to the whole class, case studies to be diagnosed by cooperative teams, or individual exercises.

Defining Features of Mastery Learning

These apparent differences in classroom structure nevertheless have the following common elements, which in research studies tend to be the defining features of mastery treatments when compared with traditional methods:

1. Explicit instructional objectives, hierarchically sequenced, which all students are expected to attain

2. Criterion-referenced assessment to evaluate and provide feedback on the achievement of those objectives

3. Remedial instruction for students who did not achieve the desired standard of performance

These have proven to be not only the three defining features of mastery learning in the research that follows but also the active ingredients responsible for significant effects (e.g., Kulik, Kulik, & Bangert-Drowns, 1990a). As we argued earlier, however, the best programs go beyond these three to include the following:

4. Enrichment activities and a corresponding grading scheme to encourage students to go beyond initial mastery of essentials to higher-order thinking with and applications of their newly acquired knowledge and skills.

Although there has been no research specific to this last point, including #4 in a mastery program addresses the oft-repeated critique that mastery helps slower learners but at the expense of faster learners.

Empirical Evidence: Overview and Executive Summary

The majority of research comparing mastery learning with traditional systems of instruction was conducted prior to 1990. Hundreds of studies have been conducted, but more important, this impressive corpus of literature has been subjected to numerous critical reviews and meta-analyses regarding the effects of mastery learning on achievement (on both standardized national tests and on local tests), on long-term memory, and on affect. Reviewing the reviews allows us to focus on the inferences these reviewers have drawn from the data, rather than on individual studies. We begin with those generalizations as an executive summary, followed by a brief explanation of meta-analysis and effect size, on which those generalizations tend to be based. Then we describe two studies as illustrative of the kinds of research included in the meta-analyses.

Having spared ourselves from reviewing studies that have already been discussed by the reviewers, we then turn to brief descriptions of mastery-relevant research that is not widely known, namely, memory by fast and slow learners and the effects of mastery programs on teachers.

Literature Reviews and Meta-Analyses

The following conclusions are based on literature reviews and meta-analyses of hundreds of studies by a variety of reviewers from the 1970s to the early 1990s. The specific studies, which provide evidence for a particular conclusion, are referred to in the notes at the end of this Appendix. However, the research considered by each of the summaries was not identical, and more important, the conclusions drawn varied at times. Of particular issue among the various authors of the meta-analyses was the effect of mastery on standardized test scores, with Slavin (1987) concluding no significant effect, while Kulik, Kulik, and Bangert-Drowns (1990b) and Guskey and Pigott (1988) concluding there was. All reviewers agree that mastery improves performance on criterion-referenced tests. We should note that Slavin's methodology differed from the others and likely could explain this difference (Slavin limited the studies selected for analysis to those studying group-based mastery learning at the elementary and secondary levels, while others included studies of other methods and educational levels).

Following are the conservative conclusions we draw from these summaries:

1. Regarding achievement,[1] both LFM and PSI are generally superior to traditional teaching/testing methods:

    a. On locally developed, criterion-referenced tests (e.g., final examinations), raising achievement at least .5 standard deviations *(SD)*, on average.

    b. On national, standardized, usually norm-referenced tests, maintaining achievement or raising it slightly (but significantly).

Thus significant achievement gains can be expected on the specific course objectives with no loss and likely small gains on the broader content covered on standardized assessments.

2. Regarding memory[2] for what was learned, students in mastery learning groups score higher on retention tests after several weeks or months, again with effect sizes of .5 *SD* or more.

3. Regarding standards,[3] the higher the passing standard, the larger the gains by those in mastery learning groups.

4. Regarding affective outcomes,[4] students taught via mastery learning are significantly more likely to self-report positive attitudes toward, liking for, and confidence in their abilities in the material taught, with effect sizes in the .1 to .5 *SD* range.

5. Regarding effects on teachers,[5] exposure to and use of mastery learning in their own classes alters their expectations, as well as their attributions, for student achievement and what causes it.

6. Regarding memory by fast and slow learners,[6] it is not rate of attainment but rather the amount initially learned that determines how much is forgotten. Thus fast and slow learners forget at the same rate once they have mastered material to the same level.

The Meaning of Meta-Analysis and Effect Size

For the reader who is not familiar with some of the specialized research terminology used above, a brief explanation is offered. To make sense of dozens of individual research studies, reviewers have traditionally evaluated those studies according to various criteria, such as size of sample, length of instructional treatment, reliability and validity of measures and procedures, and so on. These reviewers then offer their assessments of which results are sound and generalizable, based on their best judgments. Examples of such critical reviews of the mastery learning literature are those by Block, Efthim, and Burns (1989); Clark, Guskey and Benninga (1983); and Dunkin (1986).

In the last two or three decades, *meta-analysis* has supplemented this time-honored critical review of the literature. The best studies, selected by many of the same criteria mentioned above, have their data combined and contrasted statistically in a large-scale and standardized fashion to see (a) whether the various individual results have similar or different effects, (b) which variables are most potent, and (c) what is likely due to chance or needs further study. Examples of meta-analyses of mastery learning studies are those by Guskey and Pigott (1988); Kulik et al. (1990a); and Kulik, Kulik, and Cohen (1979).

An additional concept that has proven to be quite facilitative of comparing results across studies is that of *effect size*. This is calculated by subtracting the mean score of the control group (e.g., nonmastery) from the mean score of the experimental group (e.g., mastery) and dividing that difference by the standard deviation of the control group. Thus if a class using mastery learning (the experimental group) had a mean score of 85% correct on an achievement test compared with 70% for a traditional teaching/testing method (the control group), that difference of +15 points would be divided by the standard deviation of the control group. If that standard deviation were 15, the effect size would be 1, meaning that the mastery class on average did as well as a traditionally instructed student who was 1 standard deviation above the mean of his or her own class (e.g., when the average student is at the 50th percentile, 1 standard deviation above is at the 84th percentile, assuming a normal curve distribution).

The *standard deviation (SD)* is a measure of the average distance of all of the students' scores from the mean of those scores. When scores are narrowly bunched together, the *SD* is small; when the spread is great, the *SD* is large. Thus effect size depends not only on the size of the difference between the experimental and control groups but also on the range of performances by students in the control group. In the example above, if the *SD* had been 7.5, effect size would have been 2; if *SD* had been 30, effect size would have been .5.

Regarding the mastery learning effects reported in the previous section, effect sizes of .5 overall from the meta-analyses imply that students in the mastery learning classes did as well, on average, as students who were half a standard deviation above the average (or at the 69th percentile) in the traditionally taught classes.

Research Examples

The research examples described here were included in a number of the reviews and meta-analyses discussed above. We should note that because the learning standards discussed throughout this text concern elementary and secondary students, the research descriptions provided here have been limited to these populations. However, as was previously noted, mastery learning, particularly Keller's PSI, has been studied extensively at the postsecondary levels. Research on these populations was included in the literature reviews and meta-analyses discussed earlier. For the reader interested in mastery research at the postsecondary levels, we suggest Clark, Guskey and Benninga's (1983) study demonstrating that compared with those receiving traditional instruction, mastery learning students had higher achievement and fewer class absences. That manuscript, as well as Dunkin's (1986) review, also offers a number of useful citations about this topic.

Mastery in High School Science

A study by Dillashaw and Okey (1983) examined the effects of mastery learning in the area of high school science. Participants were high school chemistry students in nine multiage classrooms reported to be heterogeneous in terms of grade level, race, and aptitude. Classes were randomly assigned to one of three treatment groups, all of which received the same three units of initial instruction consisting of lecture, question-and-answer periods, laboratory work, demonstrations, and audiovisual materials. Instructional objectives were provided to each of the groups. Group 1 received only the above-mentioned instruction. Students in Group 2 completed a diagnostic quiz every third day and chose from a collection of predetermined remediation activities based on the results of the quiz. Students in Group 3 completed the same quizzes and activities as Group 2; however, the teacher randomly chose an appropriate remediation activity based on the results of the quiz. Students in Groups 2 and 3 completed up to two cycles of remediation before moving on to the next unit.

During instruction, both on-task and off-task behaviors were recorded. At the end of each of the three units, students were tested on achievement of the instructional objectives and completed a questionnaire to measure their attitude toward science.

The results of the study indicated that on each of the three tests, both mastery groups (2 and 3) had significantly higher achievement scores than the group receiving only initial instruction:

	Test 1		Test 2		Test 3	
	Mean	SD	Mean	SD	Mean	SD
1. Nonmastery	23.1	4.5	28.5	4.6	13.6	2.4
2. Mastery	26.3	4.4	31.2	4.4	14.6	2.4
3. Mastery	27.3	4.2	32.2	4.1	14.2	2.3

There were no consistent differences found between the two mastery groups. The mastery groups also demonstrated more on-task behavior than the group receiving only initial instruction. There were no effects found for attitude.

Mastery in Elementary Mathematics

As another example of mastery research, consider Mevarech's study (1985) of elementary mathematics students. Instruction lasted for 15 weeks, with all treatment groups following the same curriculum. The treatment variables studied were mastery and cooperative learning. Achievement was determined by a test of mathematical computation and comprehension (problem solving) that was analyzed to ensure reliability. There were four treatment groups of equal ability as determined by pretesting. Group 1, "Student Team Learning," completed worksheets and received instruction from the teacher when a group was not able to complete a portion of a sheet. Students were individually quizzed following instruction. Group 2, "Mastery Learning Strategy," received teacher presentations, completed worksheets, and a quiz. Those who mastered the quiz completed enrichment activities. Additional instruction was provided in class for those who did not master the unit, and they were then required to take a second version of the quiz. Group 3, "Student Team Mastery Learning," worked cooperatively in the same manner as Group 1 and based on performance on a quiz, engaged in enrichment or remediation activities. This was followed by an additional quiz. Group 4, "Control," received traditional instruction and completed a quiz at the end of the unit.

Achievement test results analyzed using pretest scores to control for initial group differences indicated that those who engaged in mastery learning performed slightly but significantly better than those who did not, in both comprehension (*Mastery Mean* = 10.6, *SD* = 2.8; *Student Team Mastery Mean* = 10.4, *SD* = 2.0; *Student Team Mean* = 9.8, *SD* = 2.6; *Control Mean* = 9.2, *SD* = 2.8) and computation (*Mastery Mean* = 30.6, *SD* = 5.1; *Student Team Mastery Mean* = 29.2, *SD* = 5.1; *Student Team Mean* = 29.1, *SD* = 6.1; *Control Mean* = 25.1, *SD* = 7.1). Furthermore, those engaged in cooperative activities did not perform significantly better than those who worked individually. There were no consistent interactions in terms of cooperative learning or mastery. Thus, specific to our interests, although there was an effect found for mastery, there were no advantages demonstrated when mastery was implemented with cooperative learning.

Conclusions From Research Examples

Two studies cannot begin to exhaust the many procedures, populations, and domains that have been researched in the mastery learning literature. Nevertheless, these studies are representative in showing significant effects of mastery learning on the local criterion-referenced tests of interest to the teachers in those classes. They are also representative in other ways: (a) Many studies include other treatments (such as cooperative methods) in addition to mastery, sometimes with separate or interaction effects and sometimes without; (b) many studies do not include standardized tests or measures of retention, transfer, or higher-level thinking; and (c) many studies do not measure attitude or liking toward the methods or subject, and if they do, they tend to use self-report measures rather than other behavioral measures (e.g., choice of method for the next unit to be studied).

On the other hand, although individual studies are usually limited in some way, the combined results from many such studies— as obtained from meta-analyses and reviews—can provide useful generalizations, as noted above. Although much more has been written about this corpus of research (see the reviews), we turn instead to some less popular, but nonetheless important, research.

Memory by Fast and Slow Learners

One field of basic research that is relevant to mastery learning, perhaps even more than studies comparing mastery-based instruction with traditional forms of instruction, is that of memory by fast versus slow learners. The general problem was introduced in Chapter 1 in terms of learning/forgetting curves, as well as what happens to the relationship between IQ and memory when a mastery standard is required. Consider the question directly (e.g., Gentile, Voelkl, Mt. Pleasant, & Monaco, 1995):

> If slow learners can be equated with fast learners in amount initially learned, then what will happen on an unannounced test of memory for that material a day or week later?
>
> a. Fast learners will recall significantly more than slow learners.
>
> b. Fast learners will recall significantly less than slow learners.
>
> c. Fast learners will recall about the same as slow learners. (p. 185)

The question has a long history because it is central to understanding individual differences in learning and memory. The earliest research on the problem (e.g., Buckingham, 1926; Gillette, 1936) produced conflicting answers because of the methodological difficulty of equating fast and slow learners on what is learned; that is, by definition, fast learners will learn more in a given time span than slower learners (e.g., Carroll's definition of aptitude). By 1954, however, B. J. Underwood found a way to solve the problem by giving students a list of paired associates to learn, but then comparing recall by fast and slow learners only on those pairs that had been equalized on probability of correctness. He concluded:

> When suitable methodology is applied to the problem, there is no difference in rate of forgetting of fast and slow learners. (Underwood, 1954, p. 276)

This also answers the above question: *c* is correct. It is not different *rates* of learning that cause differential amounts of memory; it is, rather, different *amounts* of learning. When fast and slow learners are equated on amount of learning, recall is about the same.

Underwood's (1954, 1964) procedure for equating amount learned, although appropriate for laboratory investigations of paired-associate learning, was neither user friendly nor suitable for most school tasks. Fortunately, many other researchers were induced to test this hypothesis with a variety of materials under different sets of conditions and with several successful procedures for equating fast and slow learners on amount learned.

One of the most ingenious of those procedures was invented by Shuell and Keppel (1970), who first presented a 30-word list, one word at a time, at a pace of 2 seconds per word. On the basis of number of words recalled immediately after all 30 words had been presented, students were divided into thirds: Fast learners were those in the top third of the distribution in number recalled (they learned more in the same time period), while slow learners were those in the bottom third. Ignoring the middle third, Shuell and Keppel then gave a new list of words to the fast and slow learners, but at a different pace for each: The fast learners saw each word at a 1-second-per-word pace, while the slow learners saw the same words one at a time for 5 seconds each. This procedure equalized the fast and slow learners in average number of words recalled from the list. Finally, the students were surprised with a free-recall test after 24 and 48 hours. Fast and slow learners equated in this way did not differ in amount recalled.

Gentile, Monaco, Iheozor-Ejiofor, Ndu, & Ogbonaya (1982) replicated Shuell and Keppel's results on American as well as Nigerian upper-elementary students and then invented a procedure for testing the "equal memory by fast versus slow learners" hypothesis on more meaningful material: memory for poetry. They presented each learner individually with a 10-line poem, 2 lines at a time for 5 seconds. For example, these are last 2 lines of one of the poems, by the African poet G. Awooner-Williams (1963):

Alas! The travelers are back

All covered with debts.

Students were instructed to try to memorize the poem by comprehending its meaning, not just word for word. After all 10 lines were presented, learners orally recited as much of the poem as they could while an experimenter checked off the words correctly recalled, whether in the correct order or not. This constituted one learning trial.

Additional trials followed immediately until students recalled between 75% to 90% (50–60 words) of the poem correctly. This relatively narrow range constituted the criterion for original learning, allowing trials to criterion to vary and providing a way of identifying fast (requiring only a few trials) and slow learners (requiring many). Students who exceeded the 90%-correct standard were not studied further, to help mitigate the effects of overlearning.

In this study, replicated as well by Gentile et al. (1995), the fastest and slowest thirds of the distribution tended to be quite different indeed: The fast learners ranged from 3 to 7 trials *(median = 5)*, whereas the slow learners ranged from 12 to 33 trials *(median = 15)*. Nevertheless, in surprise retention tests days or weeks later, the fast and slow learners were not significantly different in average number of words of the poem they recalled.

Gentile et al. (1995) also extended this research to ask what happens to fast and slow learners in relearning to the same 75% to 90% standard. They found, first, that there was tremendous *savings* in relearning. Fast learners, who on average required 5.3 trials at original learning, relearned to criterion in an average of only 1.4 trials. The corresponding data for slow learners was 17.4 trials at original learning and, remarkably, only 2.1 at relearning. The 1:3 ratio (fast:slow) advantage at original learning was reduced to 1:1.5 at relearning. All students, the fastest and slowest, were ready to relearn quickly as a result of having initially learned to a high mastery standard. *Such data refute the oft-heard argument that there is no time to make sure each student learns to a high level; the savings in relearning time suggests that in the long run, teachers will save time by bringing all students to a high standard at original learning.*

The data with regard to memory, however, were a bit more complicated. It happened that despite the 75% to 90% criterion, fast and slow learners were not exactly equated. While the means of both groups were in that range, the fast learners were significantly higher than the slow learners. This learning difference resulted in a significant difference in recall as well. Nevertheless, as the learning/memory curves described in Chapter 1 predict, there was much less forgetting after relearning than after original learning.

Additional research needs to be done in this field, particularly regarding the strategy differences between fast and slow learners. What seems clear, however, is that requiring mastery to a high standard at original learning accrues the following benefits: (a) Fast and slow learners will recall about the same amount and are therefore both ready to have their prior knowledge activated in the current lesson (whether it be a review lesson or new applications of the material); and (b) relearning will be faster for all, saving time in the long run.

What Are the Effects of Mastery on Teachers?

In Chapter 1, we noted that in their review of mastery learning, Stallings and Stipek (1986) suggested the following:

> The achievement gains observed for children in mastery-based programs may be explained as much by teachers' enhanced expectations, especially for the low-ability students, as by any other aspect of the program. (p. 746)

There are at least two ways in which teacher expectations might operate to enhance student achievement. The first is as a spurious or temporary boost to performance due to the novelty of the situation, the increased attention being paid to the learners, or by sensitizing teachers' perceptions to otherwise normal performances and putting a positive spin on them. These explanations are roughly parallel to the well-known placebo, or Pygmalion, effects in research. There is little doubt that such effects operate in studies in mastery learning as they do in most, if not all, human research, from drug studies to group processes to teaching methods.

But there is a potentially more fundamental and lasting effect of expectations that can arise by changing a teacher's attitudes or, indeed, their whole philosophy of teaching. Is this what Stallings and Stipek (1986) meant in their phrase before the above quotation that reads "by convincing teachers that all children can master the curriculum" (p. 746)? Whether this was their intent or not, there is some evidence for this more profound view of the effects of mastery learning on teachers.

In a series of studies, Thomas Guskey (1982, 1984, 1985) explored some of these effects. In the first, for example, 44 intermediate and high school teachers in a metropolitan area participated in a paid inservice workshop on mastery learning:

> [They] agreed to teach two classes in the same area, at the same grade level, during the school term following training. . . . One of these classes was to be taught in a mastery learning format (mastery); the other was to be taught by whatever methods or procedures the teacher typically employed (control). (Guskey, 1982)

Procedures for both classes were the same, with one important difference: The mastery class received feedback and corrective exercises followed by a second quiz.

Both before and after instruction, teachers rated their students into 1 of 5 categories, with an equal number of people placed in each quintile, on the basis of their "academic potential" or "probable achievement." Guskey then divided the teachers into two groups: those who *experienced positive change,* defined as their mastery students doing better on the tests and getting higher grades than their control students ($N = 34$) and those who obtained no such change ($N = 10$). To ascertain whether teachers' expectations were altered, he compared the correlations between pre- and postinstruction ratings of students. For the 10 teachers who found no positive effect for mastery, the correlations were about .90, indicating that teachers' ratings of students' achievement after instruction matched the preinstruction expectations almost exactly. For the 34 teachers who experienced positive change, however, the pre- to postinstruction correlation was .83 for the control group and only .53 for the mastery group. Guskey (1982) concluded that seeing students being affected by instruction alters teachers' expectations significantly.

In another study, Guskey (1985) added additional teachers, control procedures, and a self-report questionnaire to assess teachers' attributions of student success. Following mastery instruction, which involved developing formative tests and corrective activities, the teachers filled out the questionnaire again. Compared with a control group of 50 teachers (who would later get the same mastery workshop) and their own pretest opinions, the 46 mastery treatment teachers attached more importance at posttest for student success to teaching methods and student behavior (e.g., "The teacher insists that students correct all of their learning errors") than to personality or other factors (e.g., "The teacher is open and friendly").

Guskey (1984) also found a "humbling effect" on his participants' self-concepts as teachers, resulting from the successes of their mastery-based teaching. Although they had considered themselves good and successful teachers, they found that by adding these seemingly simplistic or "relatively minor" mastery procedures—feedback, correctives, and retesting—"their instruction can become even more effective and more of their students will be able to learn well" (Guskey, 1984, p. 254).

A recent study by Verdinelli and Gentile (2003) also found major shifts in attitudes by teachers after experiencing mastery learning—in this case, after studying about mastery in a graduate course that also used the mastery testing, enrichment projects, and grading procedures espoused in this book. Attitude was measured by agreement or disagreement with 12 basic tenets of mastery learning. For example, to the statement "Mastery learning holds back fast learners who have to wait for slower learners to catch up before moving on," 43% of the 67 educators disagreed at pretest (as mastery advocates would), but 82% disagreed at posttest. To the statement "When students fail a test, it is unfair to others to let them take the test again," 63% at pretest and 94% at posttest disagreed (thus agreeing with advocates of mastery learning). Verdinelli and Gentile also found a significant correlation of .38 between the criterion-referenced posttest of knowledge and posttest attitude scores, suggesting that knowledge about and attitude toward mastery learning go hand in hand.

This, of course, should not be surprising, because competence and positive attitudes toward most endeavors are mutually nourishing (or reciprocally determinative; e.g., Bandura, 1977, 1986) for self-efficacy. Likewise, their contraries—learned helplessness and negative attitudes—are also mutually nourishing, as in math anxiety or adult illiteracy. If there is a moral that emerges from this line of research, then it must concern the professional development of teachers: For standards of content as well as techniques for teaching, expectations of success can be powerful motivators for change when they arise from and are accompanied by experience with methods and materials with which students are successful (as noted in Chapter 5).

Notes

1. These findings on achievement outcomes are based on reviews by Anderson (1985); Anderson & Burns (1987); Block, Efthim, & Burns (1989); Guskey & Gates (1986); Kulik, Kulik, & Bangert-Drowns (1990a, 1990b); Kulik, Kulik, & Cohen (1979); and Slavin (1987).

2. These findings on memory are based on Guskey & Pigott (1988) and Kulik, Kulik, & Bangert-Drowns (1990a).

3. These findings on standards are based on Block & Burns (1977) and Kulik, Kulik, & Bangert-Drowns (1990a).

4. These findings on affective outcomes are based on Block & Burns (1977); Block, Efthim, & Burns (1989); Guskey & Gates (1986); and Guskey & Pigott (1988).

5. These findings on effects on teachers are based on Guskey (1982, 1984, 1985) and Verdinelli & Gentile (2003).

6. These findings on memory by fast and slow learners are based on a literature review and additional results by Gentile et al. (1995).

Glossary

Amount of Learning   In Carroll's model of school learning, amount learned is a function of time spent divided by time needed (e.g., if you need 2 hours but spend only 1, amount learned with be 50%).

Analysis   In both Bloom's and Marzano's taxonomies, processes of finding and comparing component parts to each other and the whole, examining for similarities and differences, etc.

Anticipatory Set   A prelude to a lesson that induces students to retrieve prior knowledge that is relevant to the current lesson, thus increasing the probability of comprehending it, as well as transferring that prior knowledge to the new situation.

Application   In Bloom's taxonomy, the ability to use or transfer knowledge, skills, or dispositions learned in one setting to other settings or problems.

Aptitude   In Carroll's model of school learning, the time required by an individual to learn some concept or skill to a preestablished standard (see *Amount of Learning*). This definition supplants previous definitions in which aptitude was conceived as the amount or level of complexity of which a student was capable.

Automaticity   Learning that goes well beyond initial mastery to the point at which little or no conscious attention is required but performances are fluent and effortless.

Benchmarks   Specific elements of content contained within each learning standard. These are sequenced, significant educational goals that when achieved, affirm competence in the content or skill identified (see *Mastery Objectives*). Whereas standards typically span grade levels, benchmarks (often multiple) are identified at grade level intervals (Marzano, 2001).

Bloom's Taxonomy   A classification of instructional objectives according to level of cognitive complexity involved. In increasing order, Bloom identifies six main levels: Knowledge, Comprehension, Application, Analysis, Synthesis, and Evaluation.

Cognitive Conflict   A point in the learning or developmental process at which a student confronts his or her own ignorance or misinformation about a topic. This, according to Piaget, motivates the student to want to learn, providing the optimal "teachable moment."

Comprehension   In both Bloom's and Marzano's taxonomies, the beginning levels of understanding, organizing, and representing knowledge.

Constructivist   An educational approach that emphasizes that for academic learning to be meaningful, we should attempt to make it active rather than passive, constructive rather than reproductive or memorized, purposeful rather than incidental or reactive, cumulative rather than isolated, metacognitive rather than mindless, and socially mediated rather than individual.

Cooperative Learning   Small-group or team-based academic instruction that includes (a) positive interdependence (each student has roles and responsibilities that complement the others) and (b) individual accountability (each student is responsible for learning the content). Cooperative groups often also include social skills instruction (e.g., conflict resolution), group processing, and proximity (face-to-face contact).

Criterion-Referenced Assessment   Interpreting scores or measures in terms of some standards or criteria for success independently of others, usually for the purposes of certification of competence or developing talent (i.e., teaching).

Distributed Practice   Repeated involvement with content or skills but with breaks between sessions. In contrast with massed practice, this improves retention in memory.

Domain   The specific set of skills, knowledge, or concepts to be taught or assessed.

Enrichment Objectives   Optional concepts or skills to go beyond mastery objectives by demonstrating fluency or automaticity, advanced or higher-level thinking, ability to teach, and meta-cognitive capabilities. Achieving these earns extra points or a higher grade for a unit.

Essential Objectives   See *Mastery Objectives.*

Evaluation   In Bloom's taxonomy, the ability to make judgments about the relative quality or usefulness of products or ideas with distinct criteria consciously in mind. In grading, judging student performances or products according to specific criteria (see also *Rubric*).

Feedback   Specific information on what a student did correctly, what was incorrect, and how to improve.

Fluency   See *Automaticity.*

Formative Assessment   Testing or observing students during the learning process for the purpose of providing feedback and improving learning.

Helplessness   See *Learned Helplessness.*

Knowledge   In Bloom's taxonomy, the level of processing that is mainly retrieval of specific information or facts.

Learned Helplessness   Brought on by uncontrollable failure (or unavoidable punishment), it is a state of incompetence affecting emotions, motivation and cognition (e.g., the person is fearful, gives up easily, does not master the content, and dismisses these failures with self-protective excuses such as "I was never very good in ____" or "I could do it if I wanted to, but school sucks").

Learning for Mastery   A system of mastery learning, attributed to Bloom, that is group based (to be compatible with most classroom organization), with individualization provided as needed.

Marzano's Taxonomy A modernization of Bloom's taxonomy of instructional objectives according to level of cognitive complexity as well as the amount of conscious control and centrality of belief to the person. Marzano also identifies six main levels—Retrieval, Comprehension, Analysis, Utilization, Metacognition, and Self—but in three domains (information, mental processes, and psychomotor skills) for 18 possible ways of achieving educational goals.

Massed Practice Repeated involvement with content or skills during one continuous time period. Cramming. This is often helpful for original learning, but is counterproductive for memory (see *Distributed Practice*).

Mastery Grading Criterion-referenced systems in which all required objectives must independently be achieved to receive the lowest passing grade. Higher grades are earned by achieving beyond those via enrichment activities, to demonstrate advanced understanding, higher levels of thinking or creativity on the topic, or other ways of using the skills or concepts.

Mastery Learning Both a philosophy of instruction and a set of methods for teaching and assessing, mastery learning requires that each student achieve a preestablished standard of performance on a specified set of instructional objectives in a criterion-referenced manner (that is, without regard to how well others are doing). Well-implemented programs (a) identify significant mastery objectives in terms of their necessity as prerequisites for subsequent learning, requiring students to learn and relearn until they demonstrate their competence and (b) provide enrichment objectives for students to go beyond initial mastery to expand, organize, apply, and teach their newly acquired knowledge and skills.

Mastery Objectives A relatively small number of significant concepts, skills, or thinking strategies that are essential to understanding the topic(s) being studied. Achieving these constitutes initial mastery and therefore the lowest passing grade for the unit.

Memory What remains of material or skills after learning has occurred.

Metacognition In Marzano's taxonomy, the level of thinking that involves students self-processing whether and how well knowledge is understood (see also *Metacognitive Processes*).

Metacognitive Processes Active, conscious self-monitoring of what you know well or do not know, what you recall and can not recall, what you wrote compared to what you intended, etc. Thinking about your thinking.

Opportunity In Carroll's model of school learning, the time allowed by the teacher to cover the material and induce students to learn (see also *Perseverance*).

Original Learning The extent to which students master material when first exposed to it (the initial phase of learning). Although forgetting will occur, if original learning was high, then relearning will be faster; if it was low, there is no benefit in relearning (see also *Overlearning, Relearning, and Savings*).

Overlearning Practice beyond initial mastery of content or skills. The greater the amount of overlearning, the better the retention of the material.

Norm-Referenced Assessment Interpreting scores or measures in terms of the average performance or norms (i.e., normal curve) provided by others, usually for the ranking of people (e.g., class ranks) for selecting the most talented.

Percentile A norm-referenced score, based on the normal curve, which states the percentage of people who scored below it (e.g., 38th percentile is better than about 38% of the people who took the test). Not to be confused with *percent* or *percentage* (e.g., the student answered 38% of the questions correctly), which is a criterion-referenced score.

Perseverance In Carroll's model of school learning, the time students are willing to spend to achieve instructional objectives. To the extent that students spend the time they need (see *Aptitude*), they will master the instructional objectives.

Personalized System of Instruction (PSI) A system of mastery learning, attributed to Fred S. Keller, that is individualized in the sense that students master objectives and move through a course at their own pace.

Prerequisites Prior knowledge, skills, or strategies that are essential for current objectives and therefore must be available in and retrieved from memory before learning can be successful.

Prior Knowledge   See *Prerequisites.*

Relearning   Learning that occurs as a second or later phase of the learning/memory process. Even if initial learning was adequate, forgetting will occur, but relearning to the same standard will be faster (see *Original Learning, Overlearning, and Savings*).

Required Objectives   See *Mastery Objectives.*

Retention   See *Memory.*

Retrieval   Accessing memories. In Marzano's taxonomy, the processes involved with recalling or performing, without necessarily understanding (see *Knowledge*).

Rubric   A set of criteria for evaluating student performances or products. Often, on a scale from relative novice to relative expert, scores are assigned on the basis of separate criteria (e.g., creativity, grammar, punctuation, etc.) that might also be combined into an overall assessment.

Savings   A measure of memory, the time saved in relearning over time originally needed to learn to the same standard. Savings = Time needed to learn minus time needed to relearn.

Self   In Marzano's taxonomy, the processes of identifying emotional responses, self-perceptions, and motivation in regard to one's own competencies.

Spiral Curriculum   A course of study in which immediate objectives are explicitly tied to both prerequisite knowledge and skills and more complex thinking, skills, and applications to be studied later. Thus knowledge and skills need to be mastered today so that they can subsequently be transferred in an ever-widening spiral to concepts and skills not yet imaginable to the student (see *Transfer*).

Standards   Consensus goals that students should achieve in an academic domain, along with criteria for judging whether they have been achieved. In criterion-referenced assessment or behavioral objectives, standards are the level or quality of achievement required to be judged competent.

Summative Assessment   Testing or evaluation of students as a culminating experience of instruction, as in a final or high-stakes examination.

Synthesis   In Bloom's taxonomy, the ability to assemble parts into a new, organized, or creative whole.

Transfer   The ability to use skills or knowledge in situations or on problems that are different from original learning, including being able to distinguish when or where these learnings are appropriate.

Utilization   In Marzano's taxonomy, the processes involved in using knowledge, including transfer.

References

Airasian, P. W. (1994). *Classroom assessment.* (2nd ed.). New York: McGraw-Hill.

American Association for the Advancement of Science. (1989). *Science for all Americans.* New York: Oxford University Press.

American Association for the Advancement of Science. (1993). *Benchmarks for science literacy.* New York: Oxford University Press.

Anderson, L. (1985). A retrospective and prospective view of Bloom's "Learning for Mastery." In M. C. Wang & H. J. Walberg (Eds.), *Adapting instruction to individual differences* (pp. 254-268). Berkeley, CA: McCutchan.

Anderson, L. W., & Burns, R. B. (1987). Values, evidence and mastery learning. *Review of Educational Research, 57*(2), 215-223.

Arlin, M. (1984). Time, equality, and mastery learning. *Review of Educational Research, 54,* 65-86.

Arter, J., & McTighe, J. (2001). *Scoring rubrics in the classroom.* Thousand Oaks, CA: Corwin.

Ausubel, D. P. (1960). Use of advance organizers in the learning and retention of meaningful verbal material. *Journal of Educational Psychology, 30,* 267-272.

Awooner-Williams, G. (1963). Songs of sorrow. In G. Moore & U. Beier (Eds.), *Modern poetry from Africa.* Harmondsworth, UK: Penguin.

Baker, M. A. (1999). *The effects of performance standards for learning and relearning on retention of story content by fast and slow learners.* Unpublished doctoral dissertation, State University of New York at Buffalo.

Bandura, A. (1977). Self-efficacy: Toward a unifying theory of behavior change. *Psychological Review, 84,* 191-215.

Bandura, A. (1986). *Social foundations of thought and action: A social cognitive theory.* Englewood Cliffs, NJ: Prentice Hall.

Barber, B. R. (1992). *An aristocracy of everyone: The politics of education and the future of America.* New York: Ballantine.

Bartlett, F. C. (1932). *Remembering: A study in experimental and social psychology.* Cambridge, UK: Cambridge University Press.

Block, J. H., & Anderson, L. W. (1975). *Mastery learning in classroom instruction.* New York: Macmillan.

Block, J. H., & Burns, R. B. (1977). Mastery learning. In L. Shulman (Ed.), *Review of research in education* (Vol. 4). Itasca, IL: Peacock.

Block, J. H., Efthim, H. E., & Burns, R. B. (1989). *Building effective mastery learning schools.* New York: Longman.

Bloom, B. S. (Ed.). (1956). *Taxonomy of educational objectives: The classification of educational goals: Handbook 1. Cognitive domain.* New York: McKay.

Bloom, B. S. (1968, May). Mastery learning. *Evaluation Comment, 1*(2), 1-16. Los Angeles: University of California, Los Angeles, Center for Study of Evaluation of Instructional Programs.

Bloom, B. S. (1971). Mastery learning. In J. H. Block (Ed.), *Mastery learning: Theory and practice* (pp. 47-63). New York: Holt, Rinehart & Winston. (Reprinted from "Learning for mastery," *UCLA-CSEIP Evaluation comment, 1*[2], 1-16, 1968)

Bloom, B. S. (1976). *Human characteristics and school learning.* New York: McGraw-Hill.

Bloom, B. S. (1981). *All our children learning.* New York: McGraw-Hill.

Bloom, B. S. (1986). What we're learning about teaching and learning: A summary of recent research. *Principal, 66*(2), 6-10.

Bloom, B. S., Hastings, J. T., & Madaus, G. F. (1971). *Handbook of formative and summative evaluation of student learning.* New York: McGraw-Hill.

Bloom, K. C., & Shuell, T. J. (1981). Effects of massed and distributed practice on the learning and retention of second-language vocabulary. *Journal of Educational Research, 74*(4), 245-248.

Brandt, R. (1999). Educators need to know about the human brain. *Phi Delta Kappan, 81*(3), 235-238.

Bruer, J. T. (1997). Education and the brain: A bridge too far. *Educational Researcher, 26*(8), 4-16.

Bruer, J. T. (1999). In search of . . . Brain-based education. *Phi Delta Kappan, 80*(9), 649-657.

Bruner, J. (1960). *The process of education.* New York: Vintage.

Buckingham, B. R. (1926). *Research for teachers.* New York: Silver Burdett.

Bugelski, B. R. (1979). *Principles of learning and memory.* New York: Praeger.

California State Board of Education. (1997a). *English–language arts content standards for California public schools: Kindergarten through grade twelve.* Sacramento, CA: Author.

California State Board of Education. (1997b). *Mathematics content standards for California public schools: Kindergarten through grade twelve.* Sacramento, CA: Author.

California State Board of Education. (1998a). *History–social science content standards for California public schools: Kindergarten through grade twelve.* Sacramento, CA: Author.

California State Board of Education. (1998b). *Science content standards for California public schools: Kindergarten through grade twelve.* Sacramento, CA: Author.

California Department of Education. (2002). *Fact book 2002: Handbook of education information.* Sacramento, CA: Author.

Carroll, J. B. (1963). A model of school learning. *Teachers College Record, 64,* 723-733.

Carroll, J. B. (1989). The Carroll model: A 25-year retrospective and prospective view. *Educational Researcher, 8*(l), 26-31.

Charness, N. (Ed.). (1985). Special issue on skill. *Canadian Journal of Psychology, 39*(2).

Clark, C. R., Guskey, T. R., & Benninga, J. S. (1983). The effectiveness of mastery learning strategies in undergraduate education courses. *Journal of Educational Research, 76,* 210-214.

Cronbach, L. J. (1966). The logic of experiments on discovery. In L. S. Shulman & E. R. Keisler (Eds.), *Learning by discovery: A critical appraisal* (pp. 76-92). Chicago: Rand-McNally.

DeCecco, J. P. (1968). *The psychology of learning and instruction: Educational psychology.* Englewood Cliffs, NJ: Prentice Hall.

Dewey, J. (1933). *How we think.* Boston: Heath.

Dillashaw, F. G., & Okey, J. R. (1983). Effects of a modified mastery learning strategy on achievement, attitudes, and on-task behavior of high school chemistry students. *Journal of Research in Science Teaching, 20*(3), 203-211.

Dunkin, M. J. (1986). Research on teaching in higher education. In M. C. Wittrock (Ed.), *Handbook on research of teaching* (3rd ed., pp. 754-777). New York: Macmillan.

Dweck, C. S., & Licht, B. G. (1980). Learned helplessness and intellectual achievement. In M. J. Garber & M. E. P. Seligman (Eds.), *Human helplessness: Theory and applications.* New York: Academic Press.

Ebbinghaus, H. (1964). *Memory: A contribution to experimental psychology* (H. A. Ruger & E. C. Bussenius, Trans.). New York: Dover. (Original work published 1885)

Ennis, R. (1987). A taxonomy of critical thinking dispositions and abilities. In J. Baron & R. Sternberg (Eds.), *Teaching thinking skills* (pp. 9-26). New York: Freeman.

Erikson, E. H. (1963). *Childhood and society* (2nd ed.). New York: Norton.

Erikson, E. H. (1968). *Identity: Youth and crisis.* New York: Norton.

Erikson, E. H. (1980). *Identity and the life cycle.* New York: Norton.

Flavell, J. H. (1979). Metacognition and cognitive monitoring: A new area of cognitive development. *American Psychologist, 34,* 906-911.

Florida Department of Education. (1996a). *Sunshine state standards: Language arts.* Tallahassee, FL: Author.

Florida Department of Education. (1996b). *Sunshine state standards: Math.* Tallahassee, FL: Author.

Florida Department of Education. (1996c). *Sunshine state standards: Science.* Tallahassee, FL: Author.

Florida Department of Education. (1996d). *Sunshine state standards: Social studies.* Tallahassee, FL: Author.

Florida Department of Education. (1999). *Florida's system for high-quality schools: State education goals.* Tallahassee, FL: Author.

Gardner, H. (1983). *Frames of mind: The theory of multiple intelligences.* New York: Basic Books.

Gardner, H. (1993). *Multiple intelligences: The theory in practice.* New York: Basic Books.

Garet, M. S., Porter, A. C., Desimone, L., Birman, B., & Yoon, K. S. (2001). What makes professional development effective? Results from a national sample of teachers. *American Educational Research Journal, 38*(4), 915-945.

Garner, R., & Alexander, P. A. (1989). Metacognition: Answered and unanswered questions. *Educational Psychologist, 24*(2), 143-158.

Gentile, J. R. (1993). *Instructional improvement: A summary and analysis of Madeline Hunter's essential elements of instruction and supervision.* Oxford, OH: National Staff Development Council.

Gentile, J. R. (1997). *Educational psychology.* Dubuque, IA: Kendall/Hunt.

Gentile, J. R. (2000a). An exercise in unreliability. *Teaching of Psychology, 27*(3), 210-212.

Gentile, J. R. (2000b). Transfer of learning. *Encyclopedia of psychology* (Vol. 5, pp. 13-16). Washington, DC: American Psychological Association/ Oxford University Press.

Gentile, J. R., Monaco, N. M., Iheozor-Ejiofor, I. E., Ndu, A. N., & Ogbonaya, P. K. (1982). Retention by "fast" and "slow" learners. *Intelligence, 6,* 125-138.

Gentile, J. R., & Murnyack, N. C. (1989). How shall students be graded in discipline-based art education? *Art Education, 42*(6), 33-41.

Gentile, J. R., & Stevens-Haslinger, C. (1983). A comprehensive grading scheme. *Nursing Outlook, 31*(1), 49-54.

Gentile, J. R., Voelkl, K. E., Mt. Pleasant, J., & Monaco, N. M. (1995). Recall after relearning by fast and slow learners. *Journal of Experimental Education, 63,* 185-197.

Gentile, J. R., & Wainwright, L. C. (1994). The case for criterion-referenced grading in college-level courses for students with disabilities. *Research and Teaching in Developmental Education, 11*(1), 63-74.

Gillette, A. L. (1936). Learning and retention: A comparison of three experimental procedures. *Archives of Psychology, 28*(198).

Glaser, R. (1963). Instructional technology and the measurement of learning outcomes: Some questions. *American Psychologist, 18,* 519-521.

Glaser, R., & Nitko, A. J. (1971). Measurement in learning and instruction. In R. L. Thorndike (Ed.), *Educational measurement* (2nd ed., pp. 625-670). Washington, DC: American Council on Education.

Gordon, W. J. J. (1961). *Synectics.* New York: Harper & Row.

Gronlund, N. E. (1993). *How to make achievement tests and assessments* (5th ed.). Boston: Allyn & Bacon.

Guskey, T. R. (1982). The effects of change in instructional effectiveness upon the relationship of teacher expectations and student achievement. *Journal of Educational Research, 75,* 345-349.

Guskey, T. R. (1984). The influence of change in instructional effectiveness upon the affective characteristics of teachers. *American Educational Research Journal, 21,* 245-259.

Guskey, T. R. (1985). The effects of staff development on teachers' perceptions about effective teaching. *Journal of Educational Research, 78,* 378-381.

Guskey, T. R. (1993). *Preservice and inservice professional development efforts regarding Bloom's learning for mastery.* Paper presented at the annual meeting of the American Educational Research Association, Atlanta, GA. (ERIC Document Reproduction Service No. ED 360 282)

Guskey, T. R., & Gates, S. L. (1986). Synthesis of research on the effects of mastery learning in elementary and secondary classrooms. *Educational Leadership, 43*(8), 73-80.

Guskey, T. R., & Pigott, T. D. (1988). Research on group-based mastery learning programs: A meta-analysis. *Journal of Educational Research, 81,* 197-216.

Haladyna, T. M., & Roid, G. (1981). The role of instructional sensitivity in the empirical review of criterion-referenced test items. *Journal of Educational Measurement, 18,* 19-53.

Harris-Ewing, S. (1999). *Religion, religious diversity and public education: Preservice teachers' attitudes, knowledge and preparation.* Unpublished doctoral dissertation, State University of New York at Buffalo.

Hawley, W. D., & Valli, L. (1999). The essentials of professional development: A new consensus. In L. Darling-Hammond & G. Sykes (Eds.), *Teaching as the learning profession: Handbook of policy and practice.* San Francisco: Jossey-Bass.

Hebb, D. O. (1959). A neuropsychological theory. In S. Koch (Ed.), *Psychology: Study of a science* (Vol. 1). New York: McGraw-Hill.

Hillocks, G. (1984). What works in teaching composition: A meta-analysis of experimental treatment studies. *American Journal of Education, 93,* 133-170.

Hively, W. (1974). (Ed.). *Domain-referenced testing.* Englewood Cliffs, NJ: Prentice Hall.

Holt, J. (1964). *How children fail.* New York: Dell.

Hulse, S. H., Egeth, H., & Deese, J. (1980). *The psychology of learning.* New York: McGraw-Hill.

Hunter, M. (1994). *Enhancing teaching.* New York: Macmillan.

Illinois State Board of Education. (1997). *Illinois learning standards for mathematics.* Springfield, IL: Author.

International Reading Association and the National Council of Teachers of English. (1994). *Standards for the assessment of reading and writing.* Urbana, IL: Author.

International Reading Association and the National Council of Teachers of English. (1996). *Standards for the English language arts.* Urbana, IL: Author.

Johnson, D. W., & Johnson, R. (1991). *Teaching students to be peacemakers.* Edna, MN: Interaction Book Company.

Johnson, D. W., & Johnson, R. (1995). *Reducing school violence through conflict resolution.* Alexandria, VA: Association for Supervision and Curriculum Development.

Johnson-Gentile, K., Lonberger, R., Parana, S., & West, A. (2000). Preparing pre-service teachers for the technological classroom: A school college partnership. *Journal of Technology and Teacher Education, 8*(2), 97-109.

Joyce, B. R., Hersh, R. H., & McKibbin, M. (1983). *The structure of school improvement.* New York: Longman.

Joyce, B. R., & Showers, B. (1995). *Student achievement through staff development: Fundamentals of school renewal* (2nd ed.). White Plains, NY: Longman.

Joyce, B. R., & Weil, M. (1980). *Models of teaching* (2nd ed.). Englewood Cliffs, NJ: Prentice Hall.

Kansas State Board of Education. (1999a). *Kansas curricular standards for civics-government, economics, geography and history.* Topeka, KN: Author.

Kansas State Board of Education. (1999b). *Kansas curricular standards for mathematics.* Topeka, KN: Author.

Kansas State Board of Education. (2000a). *Kansas curricular standards for reading and writing.* Topeka, KN: Author.

Kansas State Board of Education. (2000b). *Kansas science education standards.* Topeka, KN: Author.

Kansas State Board of Education. (2001). *Education priorities for a new century.* Topeka, KN: Author.

Keller, F. S. (1968). Goodbye teacher. *Journal of Applied Behavioral Analysis, 1,* 79-89.

Keller, F. S., & Sherman, J. G. (1974). *The Keller plan handbook.* Menlo Park, CA: W. A. Benjamin.

Kohlberg, L. (1963). The development of children's orientations to moral order: 1. Sequence in the development of moral thought. *Vita Humana, 6,* 11-33.

Kulik, C. C., Kulik, J. A., & Bangert-Drowns, R. L. (1990a). Effectiveness of mastery learning programs: A meta-analysis. *Review of Educational Research, 60*(2), 265-299.

Kulik, C. C., Kulik, J. A., & Bangert-Drowns, R. L. (1990b). Is there better evidence on mastery learning? A response to Slavin. *Review of Educational Research, 60*(2), 306-307.

Kulik, J. A., Kulik, C. C., & Cohen, P. (1979). A meta-analysis of outcome studies of Keller's Personalized System of Instruction. *American Psychologist, 34,* 307-318.

Lalley, J. (2003). Discovering discovery learning and other teaching methods. Manuscript in preparation.

Loftus, E. F. (1992). When a lie becomes memory's truth: Memory distortion after exposure to misinformation. *Current Directions in Psychological Science, 4*(1), 121-123.

Mager, R. F. (1962). *Preparing instructional objectives.* Palo Alto, CA: Fearon.

Martinez, J. G. R., & Martinez, N. C. (1992). Re-examining repeated testing and teaching effects in a remedial mathematics course. *British Journal of Educational Psychology, 62,* 356-363.

Martuza, V. R. (1977). *Applying norm-referenced and criterion-referenced measurement in education.* Boston: Allyn & Bacon.

Marzano, R. J. (2001). *Designing a new taxonomy of educational objectives.* Thousand Oaks, CA: Corwin.

Marzano, R. J., & Kendall, J. S. (1996). *A comprehensive guide to designing standards-based districts, schools, and classrooms.* Alexandria, VA: Association for Supervision and Curriculum Development.

McNeil, H. (2001). "Falls [sic] schools take steps toward ending grades." *Buffalo News,* November 5, p. A1.

Meier, S. T., & Davis, S. R. (1996). *The elements of counseling* (3rd ed.). Pacific Grove, CA: Brooks/Cole.

Mevarech, Z. R. (1985). The effects of cooperative mastery learning strategies on mathematical achievement. *Journal of Educational Research, 78,* 372-377.

Millman, J. (1989). If at first you don't succeed: Setting passing scores when more than one attempt is permitted. *Educational Researcher, 18*(6), 5-9.

National Commission on Excellence in Education. (1983*). A nation at risk: The imperative for educational reform.* Washington, DC: Government Printing Office.

National Council for Accreditation of Teacher Education. (2002). *Professional standards for the accreditation of schools, colleges, and departments of education.* Washington, DC: Author.

National Council for the Social Studies. (1994). *Expectations of excellence: Curriculum standards for social studies* (Bulletin 89). Author.

National Council of Teachers of Mathematics. (1989). *Curriculum and evaluation standards for school mathematics.* Reston, VA: Author.

National Council of Teachers of Mathematics. (1991). *Professional standards for teaching mathematics.* Reston, VA: Author.

National Council of Teachers of Mathematics. (1995). *Assessment standards for school mathematics.* Reston, VA: Author.

National Council of Teachers of Mathematics. (2000). *Principles and standards for school mathematics.* Reston, VA: Author.

National Research Council. (1996). *National science education standards.* Washington, DC: National Academy Press.

National Staff Development Council Standards for Staff Development. (2001). Retrieved August 11, 2002, from www.nsdc.org/library/standards2001.htmlNSDC.

New York State Education Department. (1996a). *Learning standards for English language arts.* Albany, NY: Author.

New York State Education Department. (1996b). *Learning standards for mathematics, science, and technology.* Albany, NY: Author.

New York State Education Department. (1996c). *Learning standards for social studies.* Albany, NY: Author.

New York State Education Department. (2002). *Program description handbook.* Albany, NY: Author.

Nitko, A. J. (1980). Distinguishing the many varieties of criterion-referenced tests. *Review of Educational Research, 50,* 461-485.

Palinscar, A. S., & Brown, A. L. (1984). Reciprocal teaching of comprehension-fostering and comprehension-monitoring activities. *Cognition and Instruction, 1*(2), 117-175.

Paul, R. W. (1987). Dialogical thinking: Critical thought essential to the acquisition of rational knowledge and passions. In J. B. Barron & R. J. Sternberg (Eds.), *Teaching thinking skills: Theory and practice* (pp. 127-148). New York: Freeman.

Peterson, E., Maier, S. F., & Seligman, M. E. P. (1993). *Learned helplessness: A theory for the age of personal control.* New York: Oxford University Press.

Piaget, J., & Inhelder, B. (1969). *The psychology of the child* (H. Weaver, Trans.). New York: Basic Books.

Popham, W. J. (1978). *Criterion-referenced measurement.* Englewood Cliffs, NJ: Prentice Hall.

Scheps, M. H., & Sadler, P. (1985). *A private universe* [Video]. Columbus, OH: Merrill Education Videos.

Seligman, M. E. P. (1975). *Helplessness: On depression, development and death.* San Francisco: Freeman.

Sheslow, D., & Adams, W. (1990). *Wide range assessment of memory and learning.* Wilmington, DE: Jastak Associates.

Shuell, T. J., & Keppel, G. (1970). Learning ability and retention. *Journal of Educational Psychology, 61,* 59-65.

Shulman, L. S. (1986). Those who understand: Knowledge growth in teaching. *Educational Researcher, 15*(2), 4-14.

Slavin, R. (1987). Mastery learning reconsidered. *Review of Educational Research, 57*(2), 175-213.

Solomon, P. C. (2001). *The math we need to "know" and "do": Content standards for elementary and middle grades.* Thousand Oaks, CA: Corwin.

Sousa, D. A. (2001). *How the brain learns* (2nd ed.). Thousand Oaks, CA: Corwin.

Sprenger, M. B. (2000). *Becoming a "wiz" at brain-based teaching.* Thousand Oaks, CA: Corwin.

Stallings, J., & Stipek, D. (1986). Research on early childhood and elementary teaching programs. In M. C. Wittrock (Ed.), *Handbook of research on teaching* (3rd ed., pp. 727-753). New York: Macmillan.

Stroud, J. B., & Schoer, L. (1959). Individual differences in memory. *Journal of Educational Psychology. 50,* 285-292.

Sylwester, R. (2000). *A biological brain in a cultural classroom.* Thousand Oaks, CA: Corwin.

Thorndike, R. L., & Hagen, E. (1986). *Cognitive abilities test.* Chicago: Riverside.

Travers, R. M. W. (1977). *Essentials of learning* (4th ed.). New York: Macmillan.

Underwood, B. J. (1954). Speed of learning and amount retained: A consideration of methodology. *Psychological Bulletin, 51*(3), 276-282.

Underwood, B. J. (1964). Degree of learning and measurement of forgetting. *Journal of Verbal Learning and Verbal Behavior, 3,* 112-129.

U.S. Department of Education. (1987). *What works: Research about teaching and learning* (2nd ed.). Washington, DC: Author.

Verdinelli, S., & Gentile, J. R. (2003). *Changes in teaching philosophies among inservice teachers after experiencing mastery learning.* Manuscript in preparation.

Vygotsky, L. S. (1962). *Thought and language.* Cambridge, MA: Harvard University Press.

Vygotsky, L. S. (1978). *Mind in society: The development of higher psychological processes.* Cambridge: MIT Press.

Washburne, C. W. (1922). Educational measurement as a key to individual instruction and promotions. *Journal of Educational Research, 5,* 195-206.

Author Index

Adams, W., 16, 183
Airasian, P.W., 71–72, 177
Alexander, P.A., 117, 179
Anderson, L.W., 21, 149, 168, 177
Arlin, M., 21, 177
Arter, J., 71–72, 177
Ausubel, D., 43, 177
Awooner-Williams, G., 164, 177

Baker, M., 16–17, 21
Bandura, A., 10, 168, 177
Bangert-Drowns, R.L., 21, 156,
        157, 168, 182
Barber, B, vii, 177
Bartlet, F. C., 115, 177
Benninga, J. S., 159, 160, 179
Birman, B., 143, 179
Block, J. H., 21, 121, 149, 159, 168, 177
Bloom, B. S., 6, 11, 12, 15, 25–26, 134,
        152, 155, 178
Bloom, K. C., 20, 178
Brandt, R., 20–21, 178
Brown, A. L., 75, 183
Bruer, J., 13–14, 20, 178
Bruner, J., 40, 178
Buckingham, B. R., 163, 178
Bugelski, B. R., 20, 178
Burns, R. B., 21, 121, 149, 159, 168, 177

Carroll, J. B., vii, 11–12, 21, 26, 53, 69,
        131–132, 155, 178
Charness, N., 117, 178
Chilungu, N., 97–99, 118
Clark, C. R., 159, 160, 179
Cohen, P., 21, 159, 168, 182
Cronbach, L. J., 103, 179

Davis, S., 58, 182
DeCecco, J. P., 20, 179

Deese, J., 20, 181
Desimone, L., 143, 179
Dewey, J., 50, 179
Dillashaw, F. G., 160, 179
Dunkin, M. J., 15, 159, 160, 179
Dweck, C., 9, 179

Efthim, H. E., 21, 121, 179
Egeth, H., 20, 149, 159, 181
Ennis, R., 26, 179
Erikson, E. H., 2, 10–11,
        146, 179

Flavell, J. H., 75, 179

Gardner, H., 12, 179
Garet, M. S., 143, 179
Garner, R., 117, 179
Gates, S. L., 168, 180
Gentile, J. R., xiii, 8, 21, 28, 40, 70,
        100–101, 121, 146, 149, 163–165,
        167–168, 180, 184
Gillette, A, L., 163, 180
Glaser, R., 5–6, 180
Gordon, W. J. J., 109, 180
Gronlund, N., 70, 177
Guskey, T., 21, 133–135, 141,
        157, 159, 160, 166–168, 180

Hagen, E., 16, 184
Haladyna, T. M., 7, 181
Harris-Ewing, S., 62, 64, 181
Hastings, J. T., 26, 178
Hawley, W. D., 142–143, 181
Hebb, D., 14, 181
Hersh, R. H., 146, 181
Hillocks, G., 103, 181
Hively, W., 7, 181
Holt, J., 145, 181

Hulse, S. H., 20, 181
Hunter, M., 43, 139, 181

Iheozor, Ejiofor, I. E., 164, 180
Inhelder, B., 10, 183

Johnson, D. W., 58, 181
Johnson, R., 58, 181
Johnson-Gentile, K., 103, 119, 122,
        125–126, 181
Joyce, B. R., 109, 141–142, 146, 181

Keller, F. S., 11, 15, 18, 126–127,
        155–156, 160, 182
Kendall, J. S., vii, viii, 108, 132, 182
Keppel, G., 163–164, 183
Kulik, C. C., 21, 156, 157, 159, 168, 182
Kulik, J. A., 21, 156, 157, 159, 168, 182

Lalley, J. P., xiii, 101–103, 182
Licht, B. G., 9, 179
Loftus, E. F., 115, 182,
Lonberger, R., 103, 181

Madaus, G. F., 26, 178
Mager, R., 110, 182
Maier, S. F., 9, 183
Martinez, J. G. R., 21, 182
Martinez, N. C., 21, 182
Martuza, V. R., 8, 182
Marzano, R., J., vii, viii, 26, 29–33, 70,
        75, 77, 108, 127, 132, 182
McKibben, M., 146, 181
McNeil, H., 133, 182
McTighe, J., 71–77, 177
Meier, S., 58, 182
Mevarich, Z. R., 161, 182
Millman, J., 8, 182
Monaco, N. M., 21, 163, 164, 180
Mt. Pleasant, J., 21, 163, 180
Murnyack, N. C., 21, 180

Ndu, A. N., 164, 180
Nitko, A., 5, 7, 180, 183

Ogbanaya, P. K., 164, 180
Okey, J. R., 160, 179

Palinscar, A. S., 75, 183
Parana, J., 103, 181
Paul, R., 57, 183
Peterson, E., 9, 183
Piaget, J., 10, 183
Pigott, T. D., 21, 157, 159, 168, 180
Popham, J., 7, 183
Porter, A. C., 143, 179

Robinson, N., 99–101, 118
Roid, G., 7, 181

Sadler, P., 139, 183
Scheps, M. H., 139, 183
Schoer, L. J., 21, 184
Seligman, M. E. P., 9–10, 183, 189
Sheslow, D., 16, 183
Showers, B., 141–142, 181
Shuell, T. J., 20, 163–164, 178, 183
Shulman, L., 144–145, 183
Slavin, R., 157–158, 168, 183
Soloman, P., 105, 184
Sousa, D., 13, 21, 184
Sprenger, M. B., 21, 184
Stallings, J., 15–16, 21, 165–166, 184
Stevens-Haslinger, C., 21, 180
Stipek, D., 15–16, 21, 165–166, 184
Stroud, J. B., 21, 184
Sylwester, R., 21, 184

Thorndike, R. L., 16, 184
Towle, b., 103–104, 119
Travers, R. M. W., 20, 184

Underwood, B. J., 163, 184

Valli, L., 142–143, 181
Verdinelli, S., 167–168
Voelkl, K. E., 21, 163, 180
Vygotsky, L., 10, 75, 184

Wainwright, L. C., 21, 180
Washburne, C. W., 121, 184
Weil, M., 109, 181
West, A., 103, 181

Yoon, K. S., 143, 179

Subject Index

Academic Standards Commission, 84
Achebe, Chinua, 78–79
American Association for the
    Advancement of Science
    (AAAS), 44
Analysis:
    and Bloom's taxonomy, 27t, 28
    and Marzano's taxonomy, 31–32t
Anticipatory set, 43, 99–101. *See also*
    Prerequisite knowledge
Application, and Bloom's
    taxonomy, 27t, 28
Aptitude, 12, 163
Assessments. *See also* Tests
    creative writing, 111–113
    criterion-based (CR), 6–8, 147
    development of, 110–115, 150–151
    English language arts, 69–71
    and essay scoring, 100
    mathematics, 39, 41–43
    norm-referenced (NR), 6–8, 149
    performance-based, 69–71, 116–118
    reliability and validity of, 8
    science, 47–53
    social science, 60, 113–115
Automaticity, 25, 148. *See also* Expertise,
    Fluency

Behavior:
    learned helplessness, 9–10
    and psychosocial
        development, 10–11
Benchmarks, 132–133, 147
Bloom's taxonomy, 25–29, 70,
    77, 111, 129
Brain:
    base in mastery learning,
        12–14, 117–118
    cell assemblies, 14

cerebellum of the, 13
cerebrum of the, 13
environmental stimulation of the, 13
limbic system, 13
stem, 13
synaptic connections, 13

California State Board of Education, 84
Carroll's model of school learning,
    11–12, 26, 36, 163
Cell assemblies, brain, 14
Cerebellum, 13
Cerebrum, 13
Cognitive Abilities Test, 16
Cognitive processes:
    and cognitive conflict, 10, 40
    levels, 26
    and Marzano's taxonomy, 29–33
Competence levels, 7–11
Comprehension:
    and Bloom's taxonomy, 26, 27t
    and Marzano's taxonomy, 31t
Computational proficiency, 41–43
Conceptual understanding, 41–43
Conservation of momentum, 99–101
Content standards, 87–91t, 92
Controversial topics, 57–58
Creative writing, 109–110, 111–113
Criterion-referenced (CR) assessment,
    1–2, 6–8, 15, 41–43, 47–54, 147,
    157–158
Critical thinking, 57–58
Cry, The Beloved Country, 78–79
Cultural diversity, 61–63, 78–79,
    87, 108–109
Curriculum:
    divided, 122
    embedded assessment and
        grading, 41–43

mathematics, 37–38, 39
social studies, 55–56
spiral, 40–41, 96–99

Development, 10–11
Dialogical thinking, 57–58
Discovery as a teaching
    method, 101–103
Distributed practice, 4, 24
Distribution and consumption
    lessons, 63, 65–66

Effect size, 15, 158–168
Empirical base, 15–17
English language arts:
    and breadth of exposure to
        literature, 67
    and creative writing,
        109–110, 111–113
    and development of skills, 68
    and dimensions of writing, 72e
    and English vocabulary usage, 73e
    essay scoring, 100–101
    implementing standards for, 75–81
    and inquiry via literature, 78–79, 81
    and learning how to learn, 71, 74–75
    lesson planning, 100–101, 109–110
    performance-based assessment *vs.*
        machine-scored tests in, 69–71
    portfolios as demonstrations of
        mastery, 80, 112
    and productive uses or purposes of
        literacy, 67
    and the promotion of equity and
        excellence for all, 68–69
    and quality of research, 72–73e
    and quality of story, 73e
    reading and comprehension
        standards, 91–92t
    rubrics, 71, 72–74e
    and spelling mastery, 111–113
    standards overview, 67–68, 91–92t
    teaching methods, 109–110
    and teaching reading
        strategies, 76–78
    and writing mechanics, 73–74e
Enrichment activities for mastery
    learning, 18–19, 60, 92, 94–95, 112,
    122, 125–126, 132, 148, 151, 156
Environmental stimulation and
    the brain, 13
Equity in standards, 35–37, 44–45, 58,
    60, 68–69, 84, 85–86t, 151–152

Errors in using mastery learning
    techniques, 2
Essay scoring, 70–71, 100–101
Evaluation, and Bloom's
    taxonomy, 27t, 28
Expertise, 5, 7, 116–117

Fast vs. slow learners, 12, 16–18,
    162–165
Feedback, 39, 60, 109–110,
    117, 148, 151
Fluency, 5, 38
Fractions, teaching, 40–41, 96–99,
    137–139
Franklin, Ben, 56

Geometry, 39
Grading systems for mastery learning,
    18–19, 42–43, 52–53, 59–60, 64,
    71–74, 80, 125–129, 147–150
    curriculum-embedded
        mathematics, 41–43
    and essay scoring, 100–101
    and passing standards, 124–125
    in science, 52–53e
    in social studies, 59–60, 64–65e

Hawthorne effects, 15–16
Helplessness, learned, 9–10

Identity crises, 10–11
Illinois Learning Standards, 84
Information and Marzano's
    taxonomy, 30
Inoculation theory of mastery, 24
Inquiry, 46–60, 88–89t, 113–114
Institute of Medicine, 44
Instructional sensitivity, 7–8
Intelligence quotients (IQ), 7
    correlation with memory,
        16–17, 162–165
International Reading Association
    (IRA), 67, 135

Knowledge:
    and Bloom's taxonomy, 26, 27t
    Marzano's domains of, 30
    prerequisite, 99–101, 123
    teacher, 144–146

Learned helplessness, 5, 9–10
Learning:
    amount, 3–5, 11–12, 158

assessment, 5–8, 6–8, 39,
47–53, 69–71
brain based, 12–14
distributed practice for, 4
empirical base, 15–17
and enrichment, 18–19, 60, 92–95
forgetting curves, 5, 6f
how to learn, 71, 74–75
massed practice for, 4
measurement base, 5–8
and memorization, 2–3
original phase, 3–4
and peer tutoring, 93–94
prerequisites, 3–5
rate, 11–12, 19, 158, 162–165
readiness, 3
and remediation, 92–95
sequencing of, 28–29
theoretical bases of, 9–12
time spent, 11–12
Learning for mastery (LFM), 11, 15,
155–156, 158
Learning/memory base, 2–5,
16, 162–165
Lessons:
clearly written and distributed
objectives for, 108–110
contextualized in a spiral
curriculum, 96–99
and developing
assessments, 110–115
English language arts, 100–101
and essay scoring, 100–101
logically ordered, 122–123
and the mastery philosophy, 95–96
mathematics, 96–99, 122
and prerequisite knowledge, 99–101
remediation, 115–118
science, 99–100
social studies, 108–109, 122–123
and the Suzuki Method, 97–99
taught using varieties of
methods, 101–108
Levels of competence, 7–8
Lewis and Clark expedition, 103–105
Limbic system, 13
Literature, inquiry via, 78–79, 81
Lowe, Edith, 26

Marzano taxonomy, 29–33, 70, 75,
77, 127
Massed practice, 4
Mastery learning:

adoption by teachers and schools, 2
approaches, 155–156
assessment and feedback for,
39, 110–115, 150–151
as a beginning, 24–25, 43, 147
brain base, 12–14, 117–118
and critical thinking, 57–58
decisions, 7–8
defining features of, 15–16, 156–157
divided curriculum for, 122
effects on teachers, 165–168
empirical base, 15–17
empirical evidence on, 157–160
in English language arts, 68–81
enrichment activities, 18–19, 92–95,
112, 122, 125–126, 148, 151
errors in using, 2, 131–135
establishing passing standards for,
124–125
and fluency, 38
foundations, 2
grading systems, 18–19,
128–129, 147–150
and implementation of
standards, 39–43
implementing, 121–129
improving conceptions of, 132–133
and initial mastery, 24–25, 146
inoculation theory of, 24
learning/memory base, 2–5, 16–17
logically ordered units for, 122–123
and mastery as a pretest, 43
in mathematics, 35–39, 122–129,
161–162
measurement base, 5–8
meta-analysis of, 158–160
misinformation about, 133–135
and moving on to the next unit,
127–128
opposition to, 18–20
parallel tests for each objective,
123–124
and peer tutoring, 93–94, 112
planning lessons using six elements
of, 95–118, 121–129
poorly implemented, 132–133
practice tests for, 127
and prerequisite knowledge,
37–38, 123
and professional development,
144–146, 146–152
and remediation, 92–95, 115–118, 127
research on, 157–160, 160–162

in science, 45–54, 160–161
selecting objectives for, 150
in social studies, 57–66
teacher education, 121–129
teaching methods, 95–118, 151–152
teaching to the objectives for,
        126–127
test scheduling, 127
theoretical bases, 9–12
Mathematics:
    assessment and feedback, 39
    and capacity of all children to
        learn, 36–37
    curriculum, 37–38
    and curriculum-embedded
        assessment and grading, 41–43
    fluency, 38
    implementing standards for, 39–43,
        138–139
    and learned helplessness, 9–10
    lessons, 96–99, 105–108, 122
    and Marzano's taxonomy, 30, 31–33t
    and mastery as a pretest, 43
    and mastery learning, 34–39, 122–129
    passing standards, 124
    prerequisite knowledge for,
        37–38, 123
    reasoning and problem solving
        standards, 89–90t
    research on mastery learning
        in, 161–162
    standards overview, 34–35,
        83–84, 89–90t
    teacher content
        preparation, 136–139
    and teaching fractions, 40–41,
        96–99, 137–139
    teaching methods, 105–108
    and transfer theories, 40–41
Measurement base:
    and criterion-based (CR)
        assessment, 6–8
    and individual scores, 7
    and instructional sensitivity, 7–8
    and levels of competence, 7–8
    and norm-referenced (NR)
        assessment, 6–8
    reliability and validity, 8
    and score ranking, 7
Memory, 2–5, 16
    correlation with intelligence,
        16–17, 162–165
    by fast and slow learners, 162–165
Mental processes, 30

Meta-analysis of mastery learning,
        15, 158–160
Metacognitive processes:
    and English language arts, 75, 77,
        80–81
    and Marzano's taxonomy,
        30t, 32–33t
Multiplication facts, 2–3

National Academy of Engineering, 44
National Academy of Sciences, 44
National Center for History in the
        Schools, 84
National Council for the Accreditation
        of Teacher Education, 135–136
National Commission on Excellence in
        Education, 44
National Council for the Social Studies
        (NCSS), 55–56, 60, 83, 122, 135
National Council of Teachers of English
        (NCTE), 67–68, 84, 135
National Council of Teachers of
        Mathematics (NCTM), 34–43,
        44, 60, 83
National History Standards, 84
National Research Council (NRC),
        44–45, 135, 136–137
National Science Education Standards,
        26, 44–45, 84
National Science Teachers
        Association, 44
Nation at Risk, A, 44
New York State Standards for Social
        Studies, 84
Norm-referenced (NR) assessment,
        6–8, 149, 158

Objectives, instructional, 15, 95, 108–110,
        121–123, 131, 150, 156
Opportunity to learn, 12, 53, 58
Oregon Trail, The (software), 103–104
Original learning phase, 3–4
Overlearning, 4, 24, 116–118, 146–147

Paton, Alan, 78–79
Peer tutoring, 93–94, 112
Perseverance in learning, 12, 53
Personalized System of Instruction
        (PSI), 11, 15, 126–127, 155–156, 158
Physical, artistic, and mental
        skills, 116–118
Portfolios, language arts, 80, 112, 115
Practice:
    distributed, 4, 24, 146

and neural connections, 14
tests, 127
Prayer in schools, 64–65e, 108–109,
123, 125–126
Prerequisite knowledge, 99–101, 123
*Principles and Standards for School
Mathematics*, 34–43, 39, 41
Private Universe, A, 139
Professional development:
for mastery learning, 146–152
and mastery learning effects on
teachers, 165–168
misinformation about mastery
learning in, 133–135
and the National Council for
Accreditation of Teacher
Education, 135–141
recommendations, 141–143
reforming, 135–136
science and math, 136–141
teacher perceptions of, 143–144
Psychomotor skills, 30
Psychosocial development, 10–11

Readiness, learning, 3
Reading, teaching strategies for,
76–78, 117
Relearning, 3–5. *See also* Overlearning
Religion, 61–63, 64–65e, 108–109
Remediation, 92–95, 115–118, 127, 156
Research on mastery learning,
157–160, 160–162
Retrieval, 31t
Rollerblades and conservation of
momentum, 99–101
Rubrics, 42–43, 52–53, 56–60, 71–74

Savings, 4–5
Science:
assessment, 47–53
and Bloom's taxonomy, 25–28
and discovery, 101–103
hands-on and minds-on, 45–47
implementing standards for, 53–54,
136–137, 139–141
and inquiry, 46–60, 88–89t
lessons, 48–50e, 99–100
research on mastery learning
in, 160–161
standards overview, 44–45, 88–89t
teacher content preparation, 139–141
teaching methods, 101–103
Science Standards, 27–28, 44–54
Self-system cognitive processes, 30t, 33t

Sequencing, 28–29
Shaw, George Bernard, 145
Social studies:
assessments, 60, 113–115
and cultural diversity,
61–63, 108–109
curriculum, 55–56
enrichment activities, 125–126
grading, 59–60, 64–65e
implementing standards for, 61–66
lessons on distribution and
consumption, 63, 65–66, 122–123
passing standards, 125
and religion, 61–63, 64–65e
and school prayer, 64–65e, 108–109,
123, 125–126
software, 103–105
standards overview, 55–56,
83–84, 87–88t
teaching critical thinking via
controversial topics in,
57–58, 108–109
teaching methods, 103–105,
108–109
and universal human rights,
113–115
Software, 103–105
Spelling, 111–113
Spiral curriculum, 40–41, 96–99, 150
Staff development. *See* Professional
development
Standards:
beyond mastery, 25–32, 81
and Bloom's taxonomy, 25–29
content, 87–91t, 92
development of, 23–24
English language arts, 67–81, 91–92t
establishing passing, 124–125
implementing, 39–43, 53–54, 61–66,
75–81, 121–129
and the Marzano taxonomy, 29–33
and mastery as a beginning, 24–25,
43, 151–152
mathematics, 34–43, 89–90t
overlap among state and
national, 83–92
and peer tutoring, 93–94
professional development,
136–137
science, 44–54, 88–89t
social studies, 55–66,
87–88t, 108–109
*Standards for the English Language
Arts*, 67, 90

State and national standards
   overlap, 83–92
Suzuki Method for mastering
   violin, 97–99
Synaptic connections, 13
Synthesis, and Bloom's taxonomy,
   27t, 28

Teaching methods:
   for all children, 151–152
   creative writing, 109–110
   discovery, 101–103
   and recognizing possibilities,
      105–108
   science, 101–103
   social studies, 103–105, 108–109
   and traveling like Lewis and Clark
      via software, 103–105
Tests. *See also* Assessments
   parallel forms of, 123–124, 150–151

practice, 127
scheduling, 127
scores, 7, 69–71
Theoretical bases:
   and Carroll's model of school
      learning, 11–12
   learned helplessness, 9–10
   and psychosocial development,
      10–11
Things Fall Apart, 78–79, 81
Time needed to learn, 11–12
Time spent learning, 11–12
Transfer, 40–41, 96–99

U. S. Department of Education, 67
Universal human rights, 113–115
Utilization, 32t

Violin, Suzuki Method for mastering,
   97–99